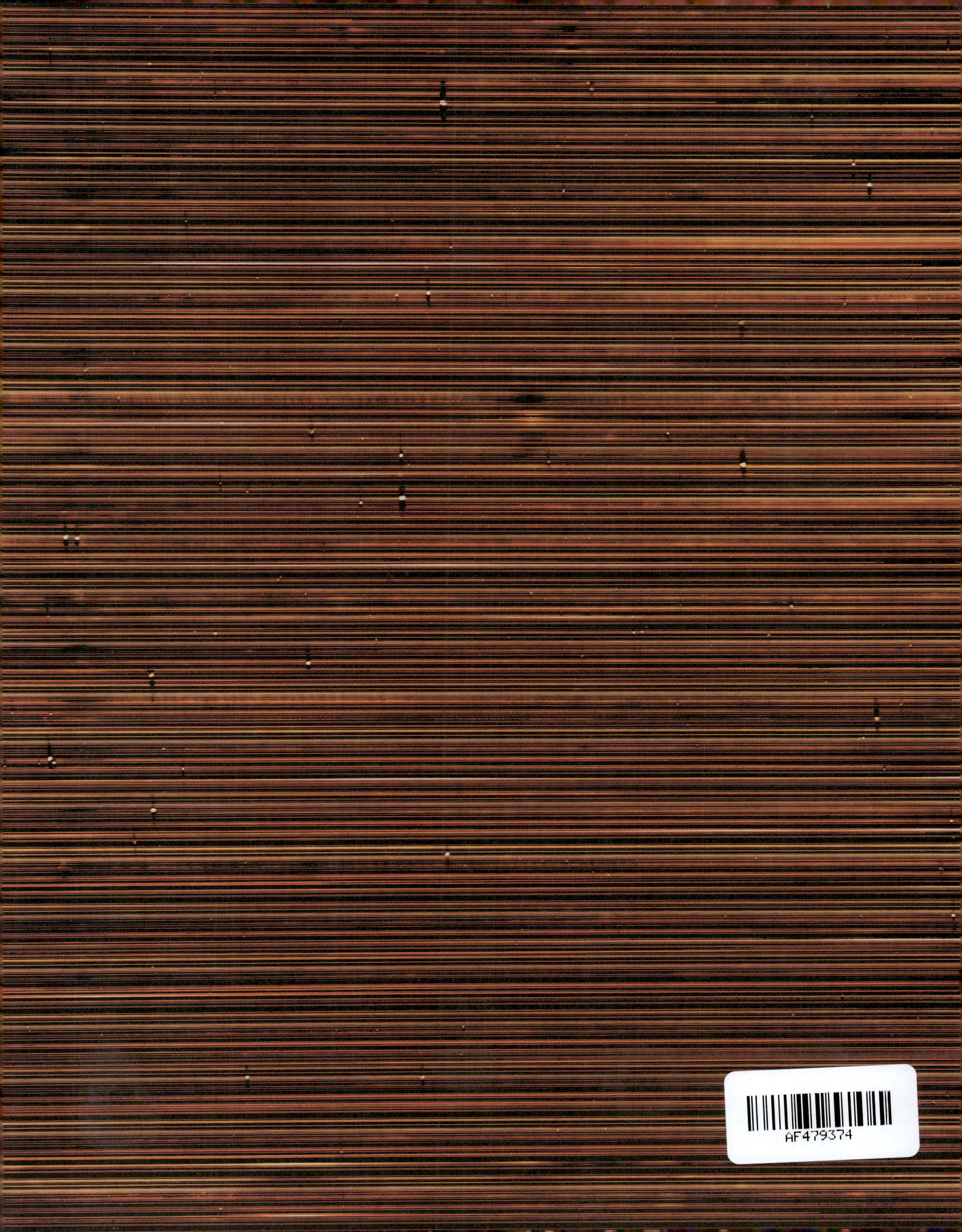
AF479374

MARCO BREUER

MARCO BREUER EARLY RECORDINGS

with an essay by Mark Alice Durant

aperture

PLATES

EXTRACTIONS

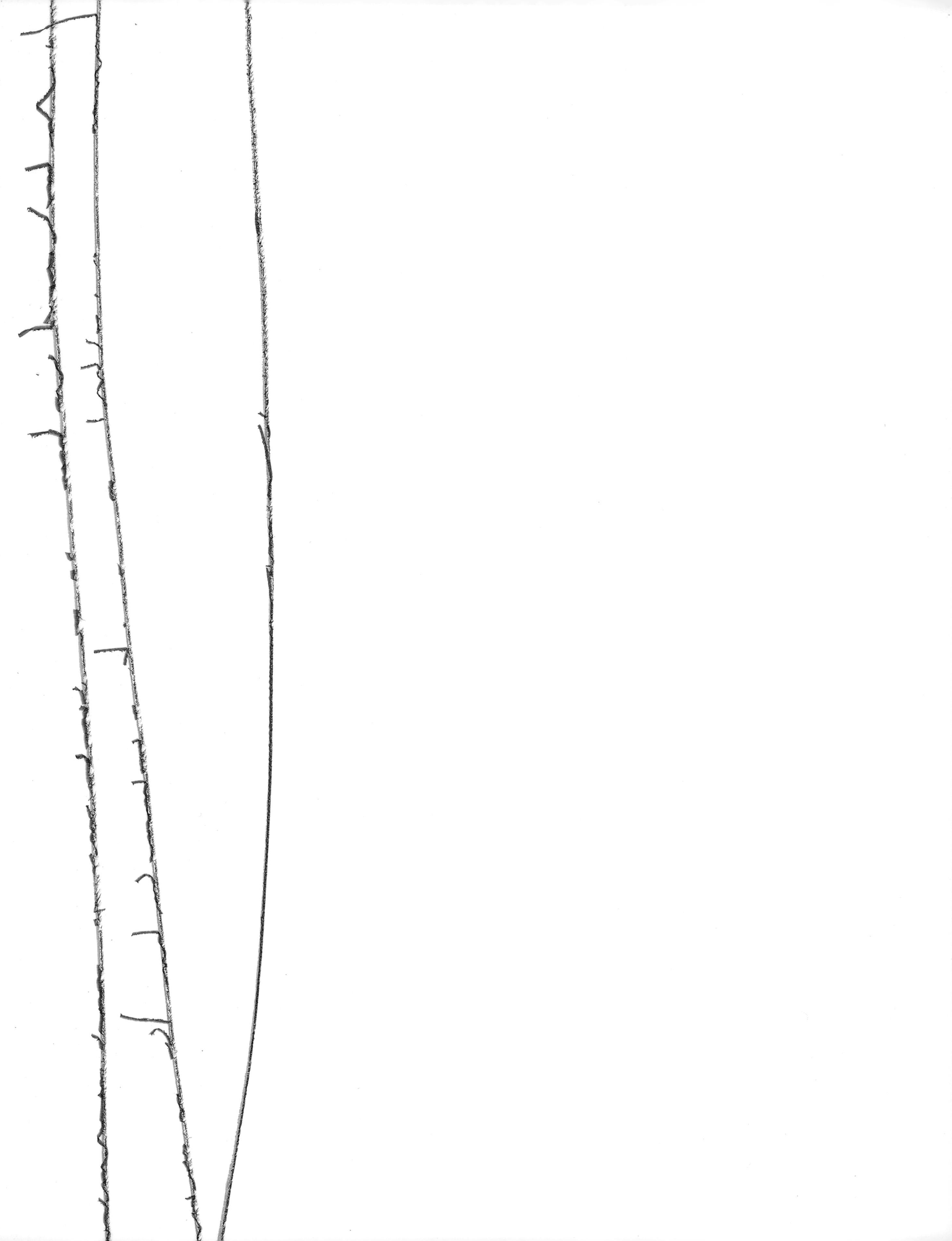

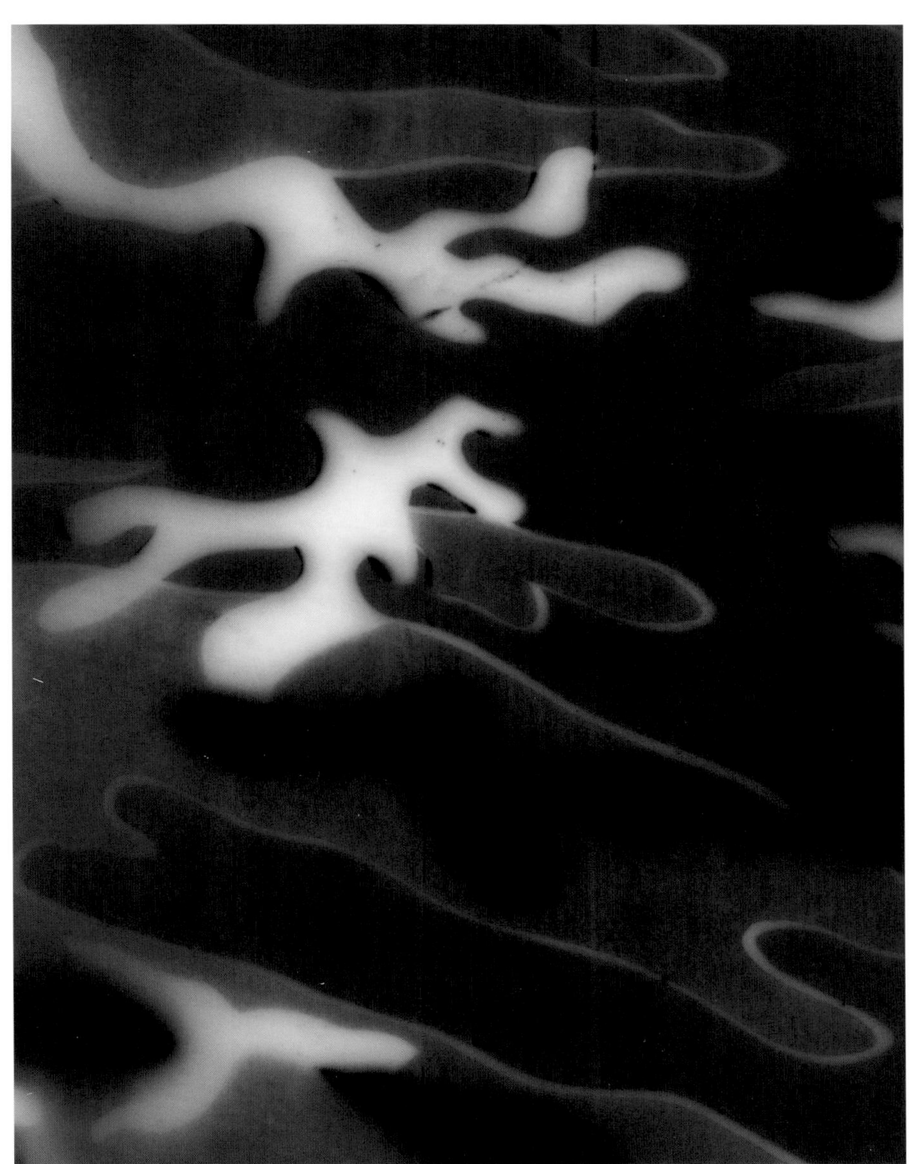

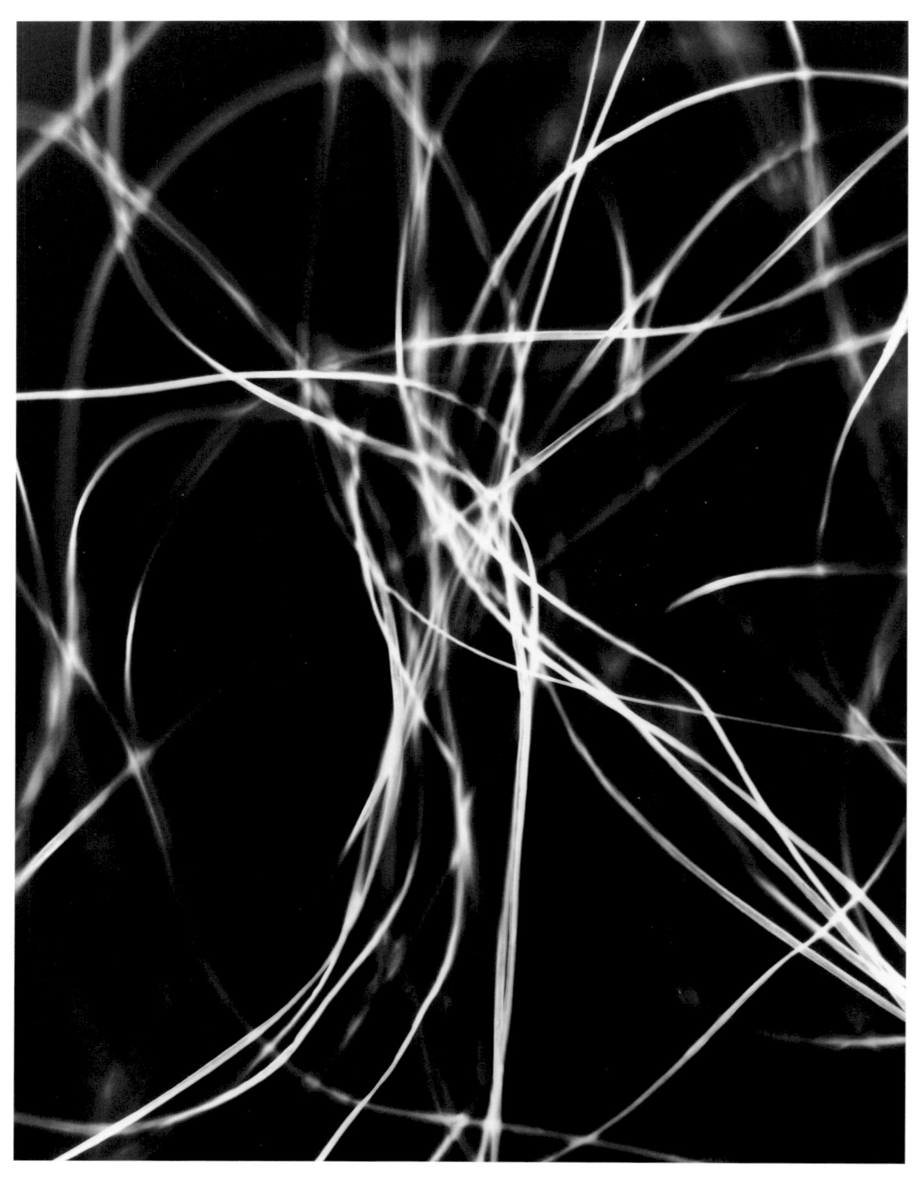

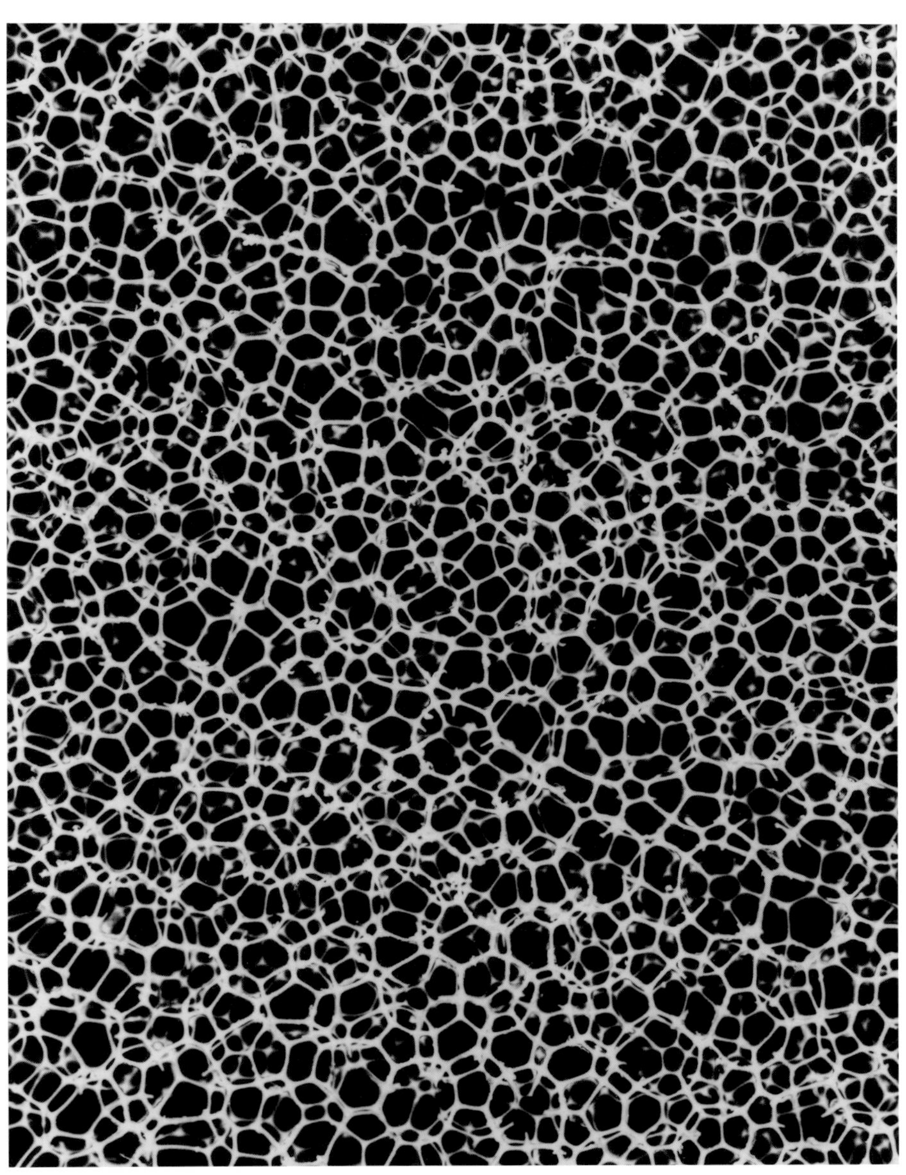

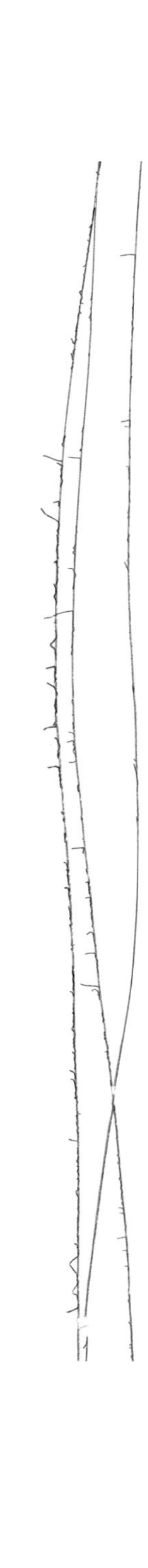

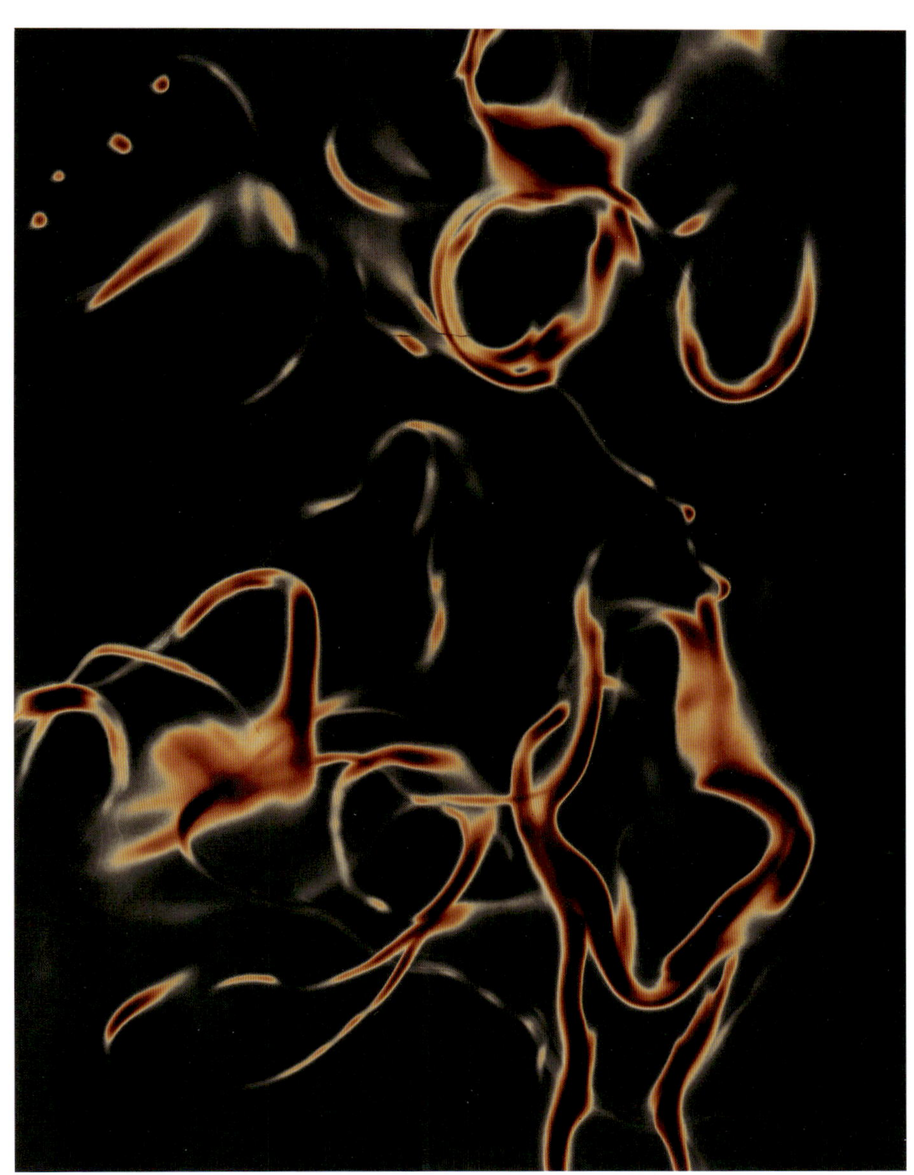

E/Z

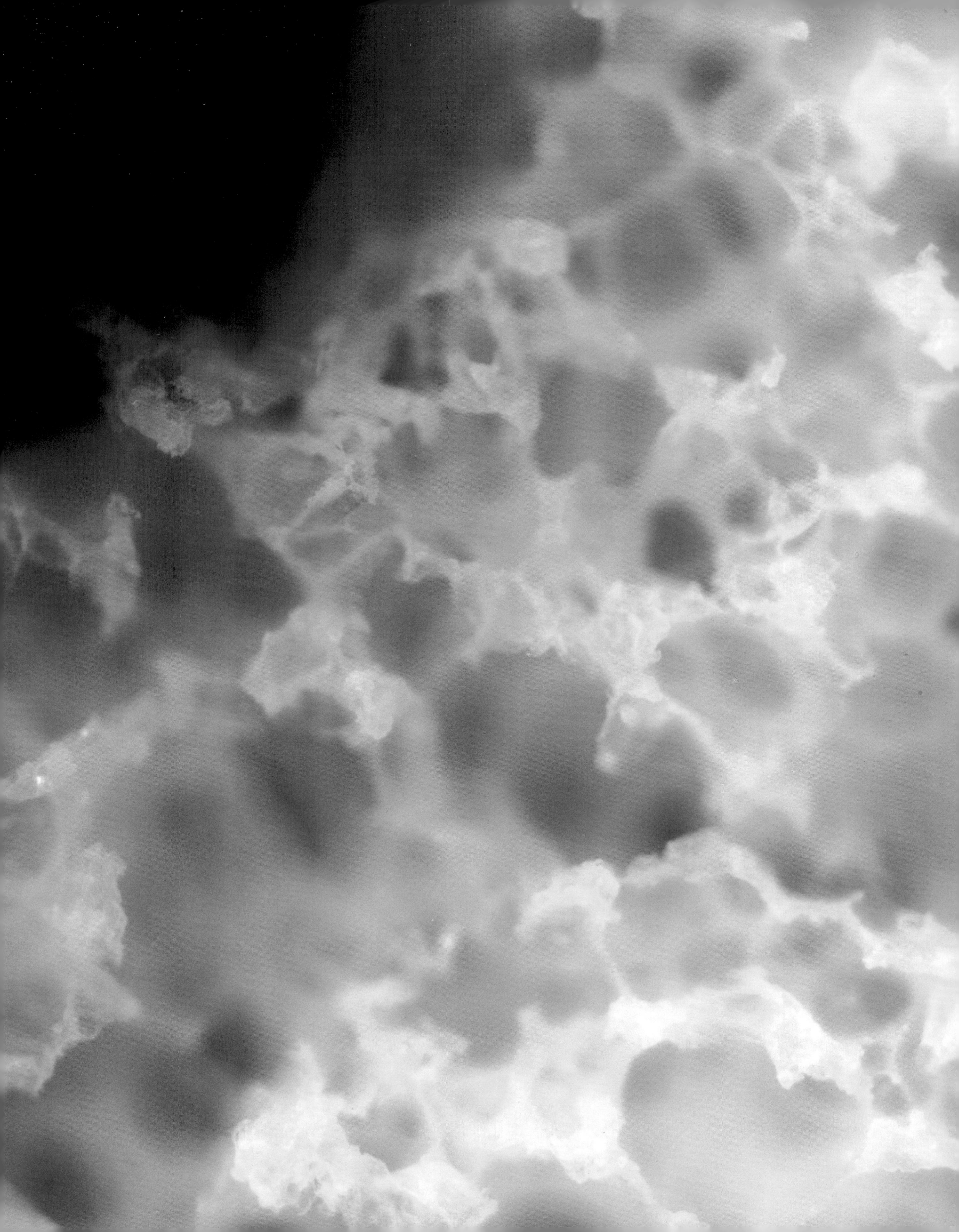

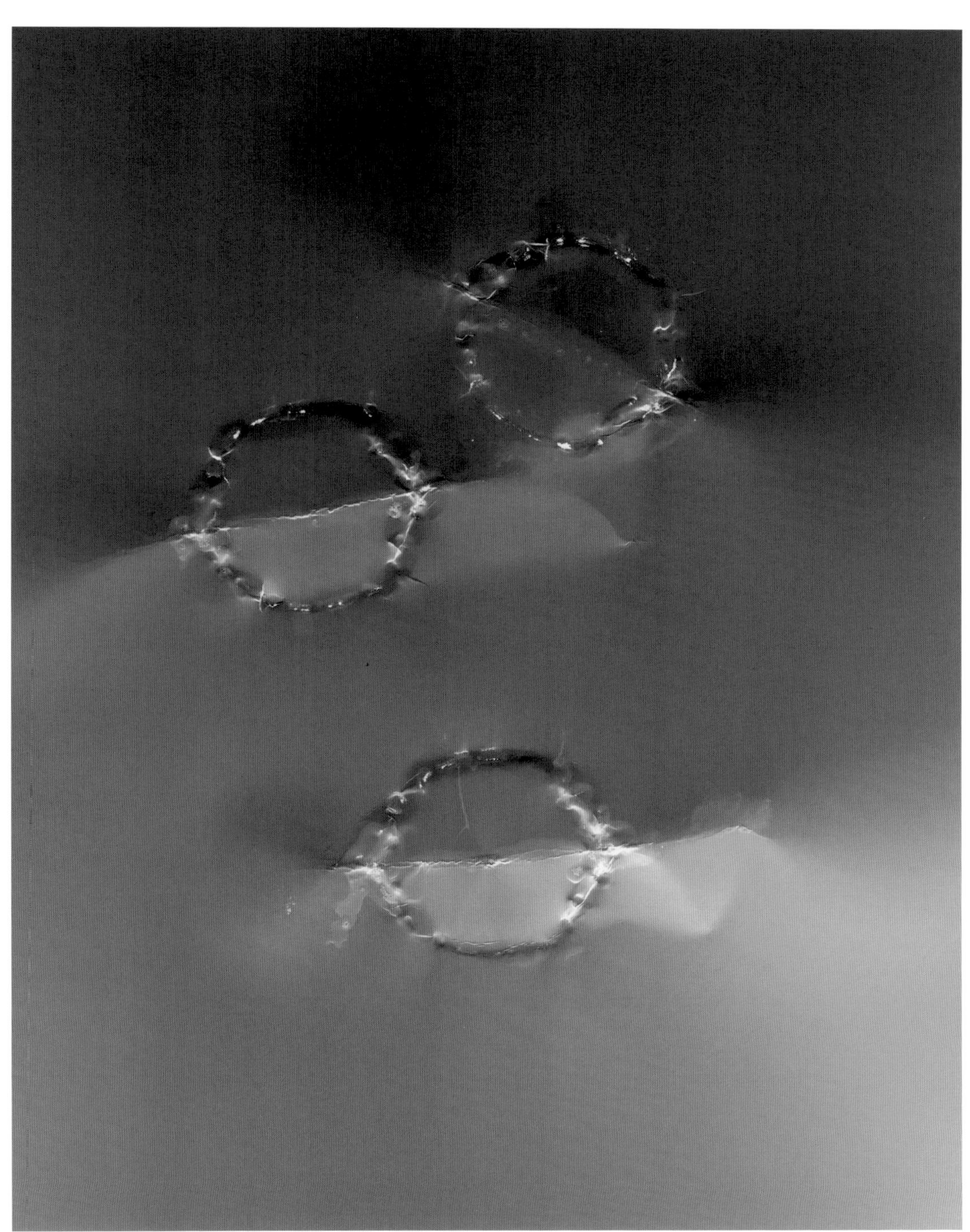

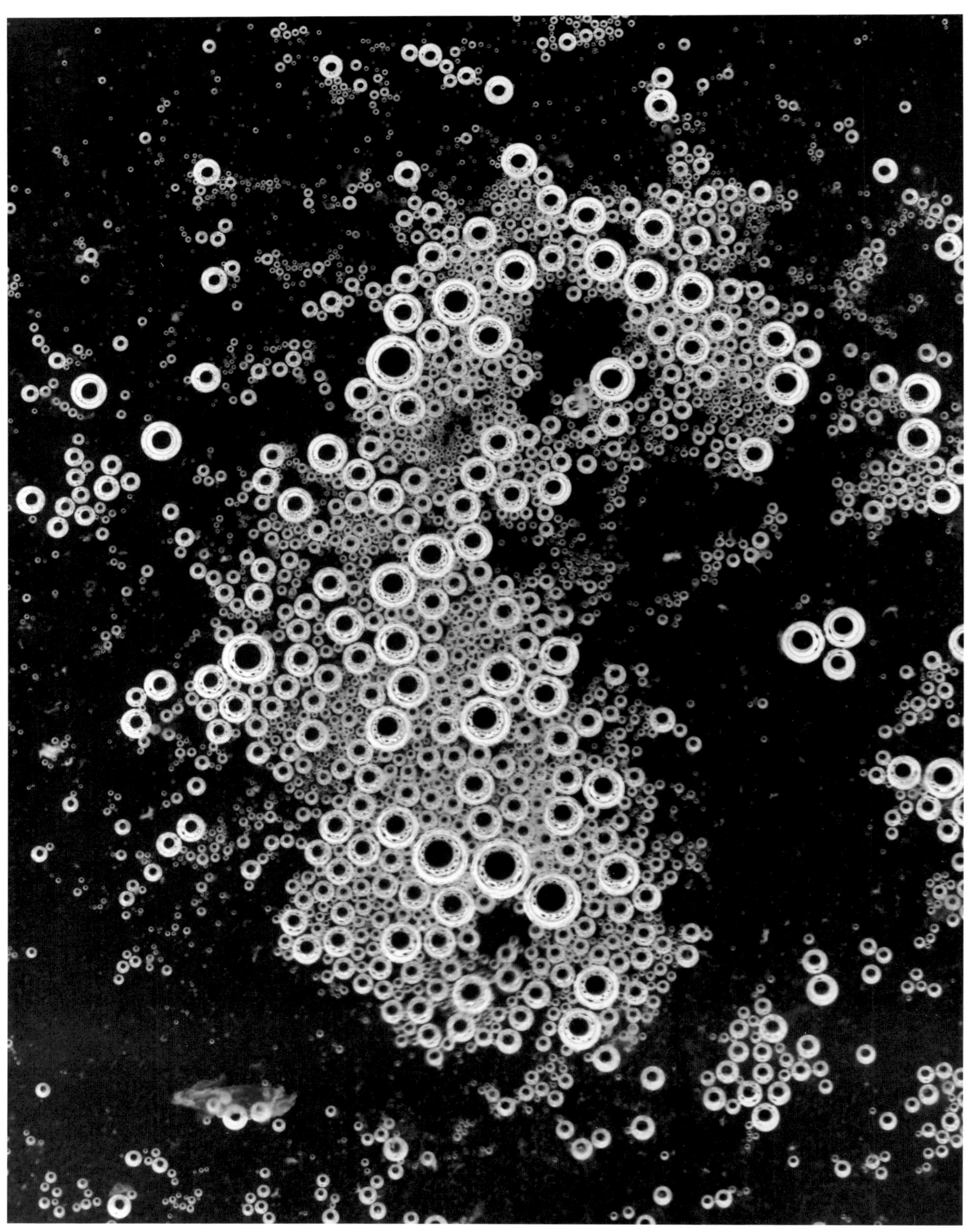

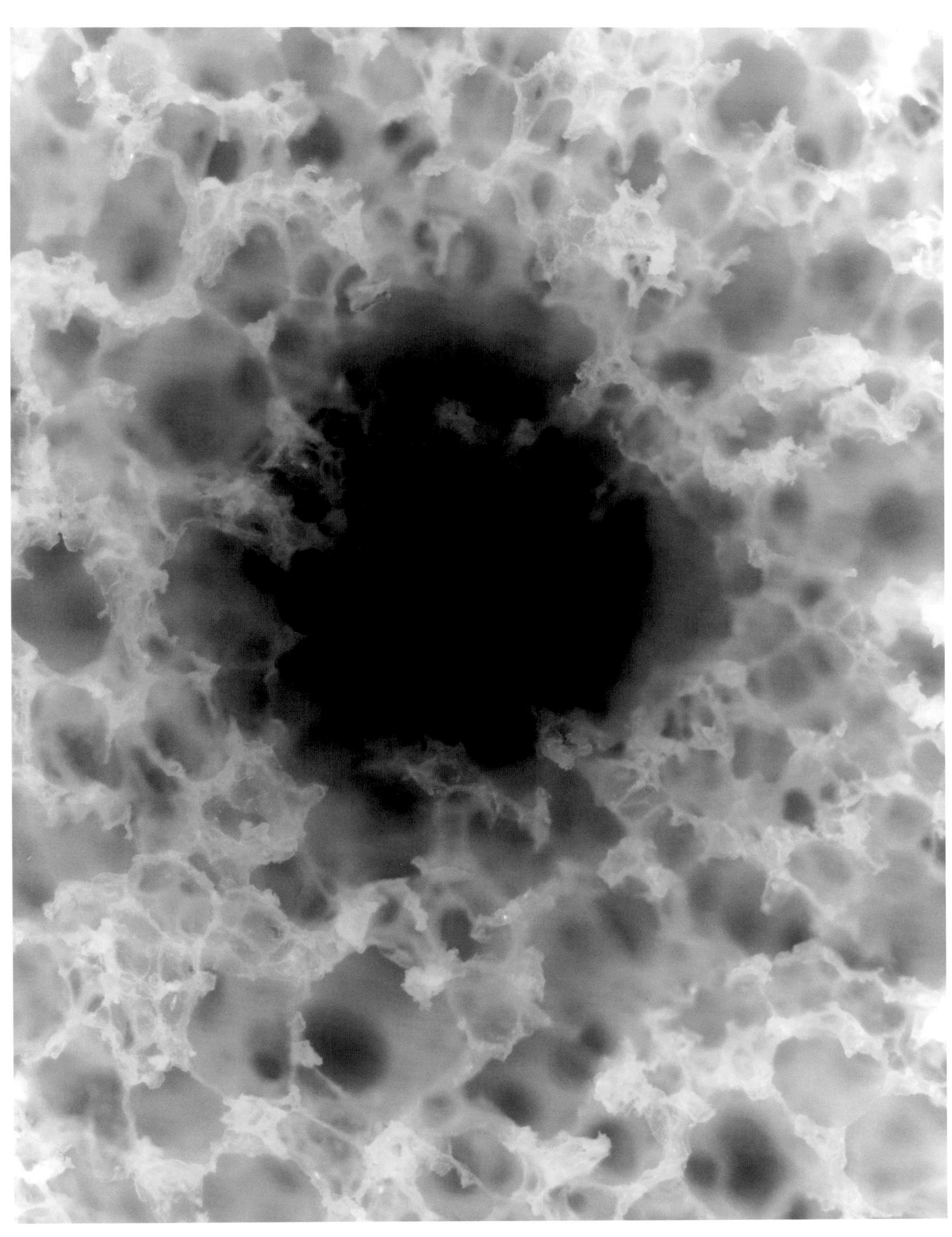

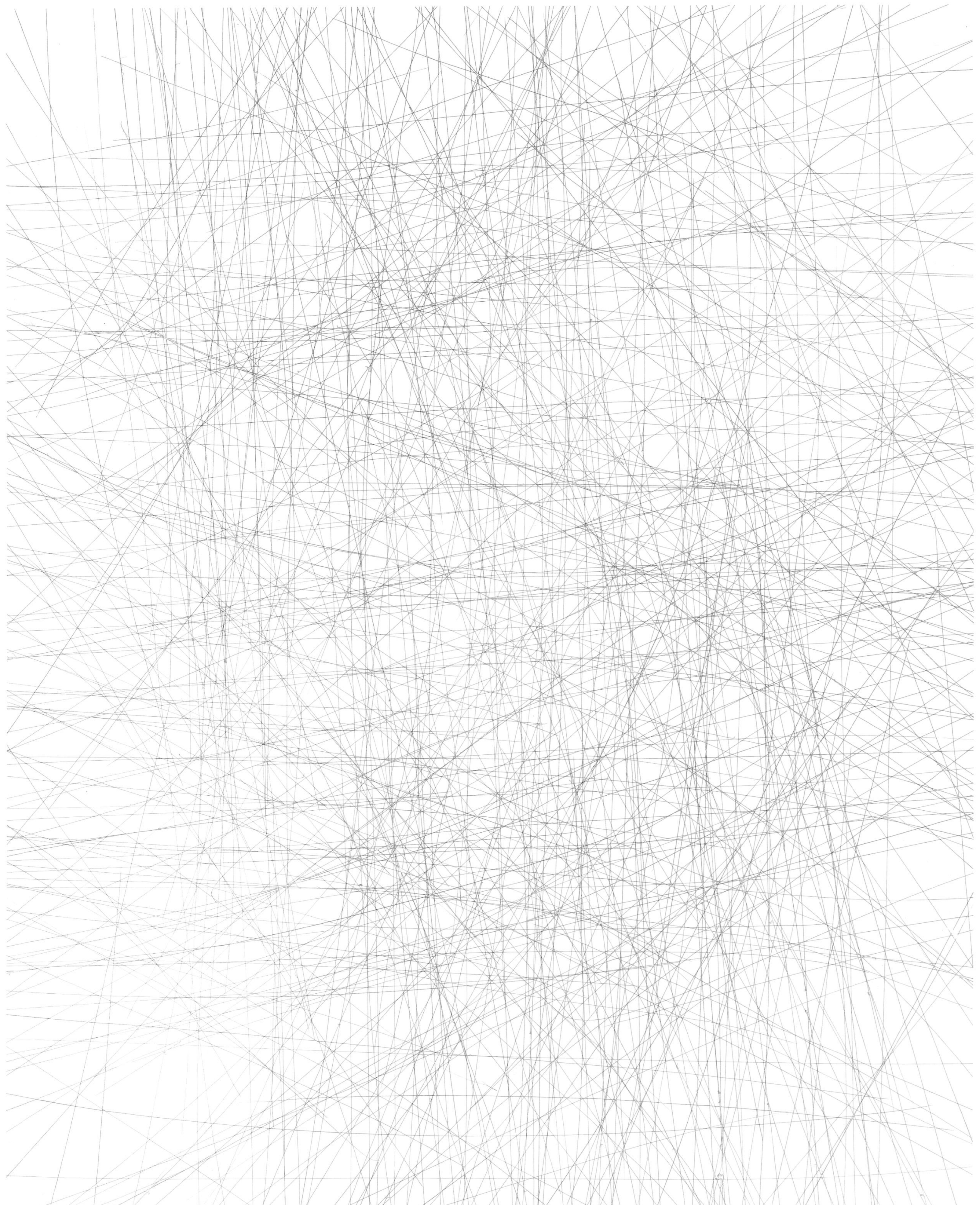

PRESENT TENSE

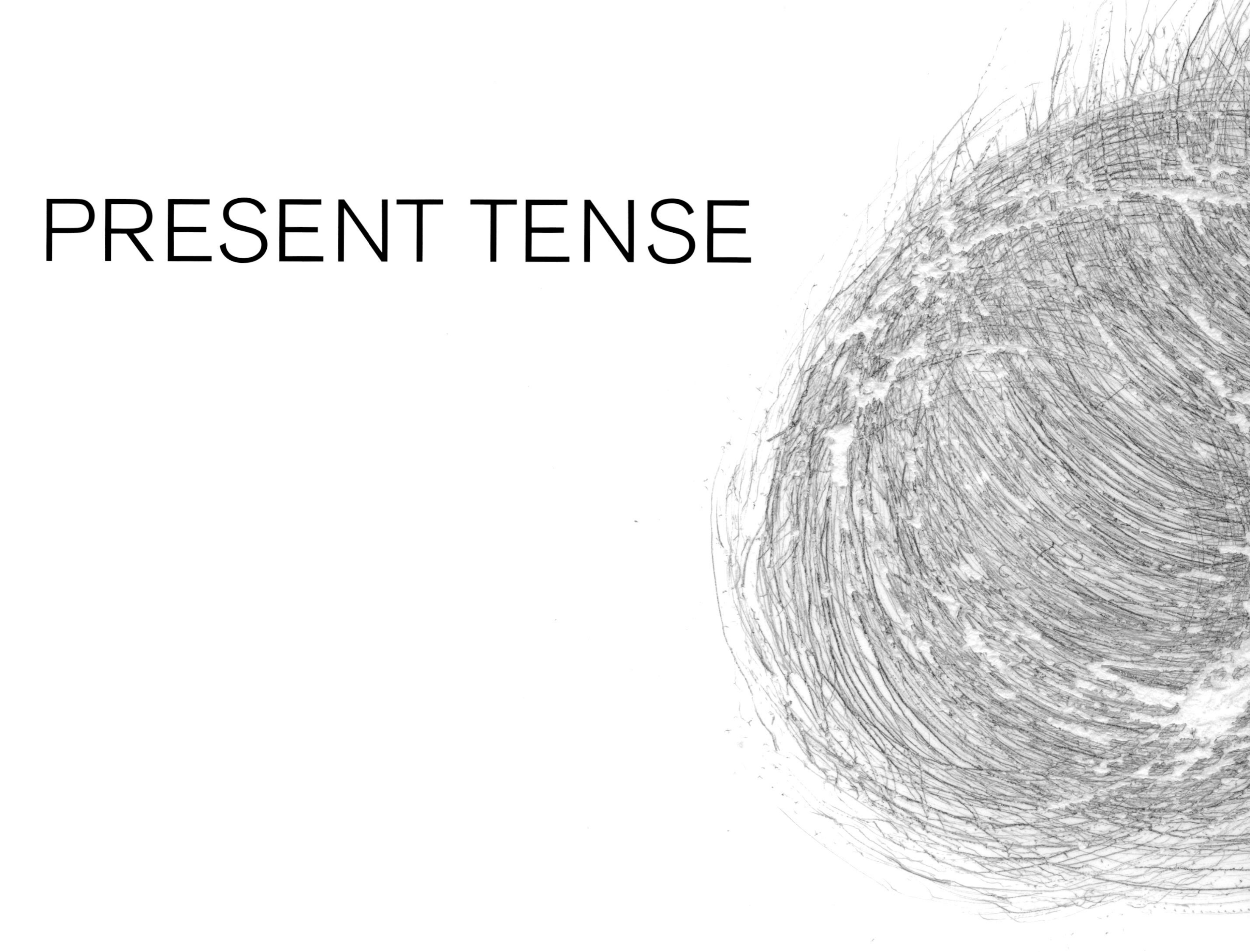

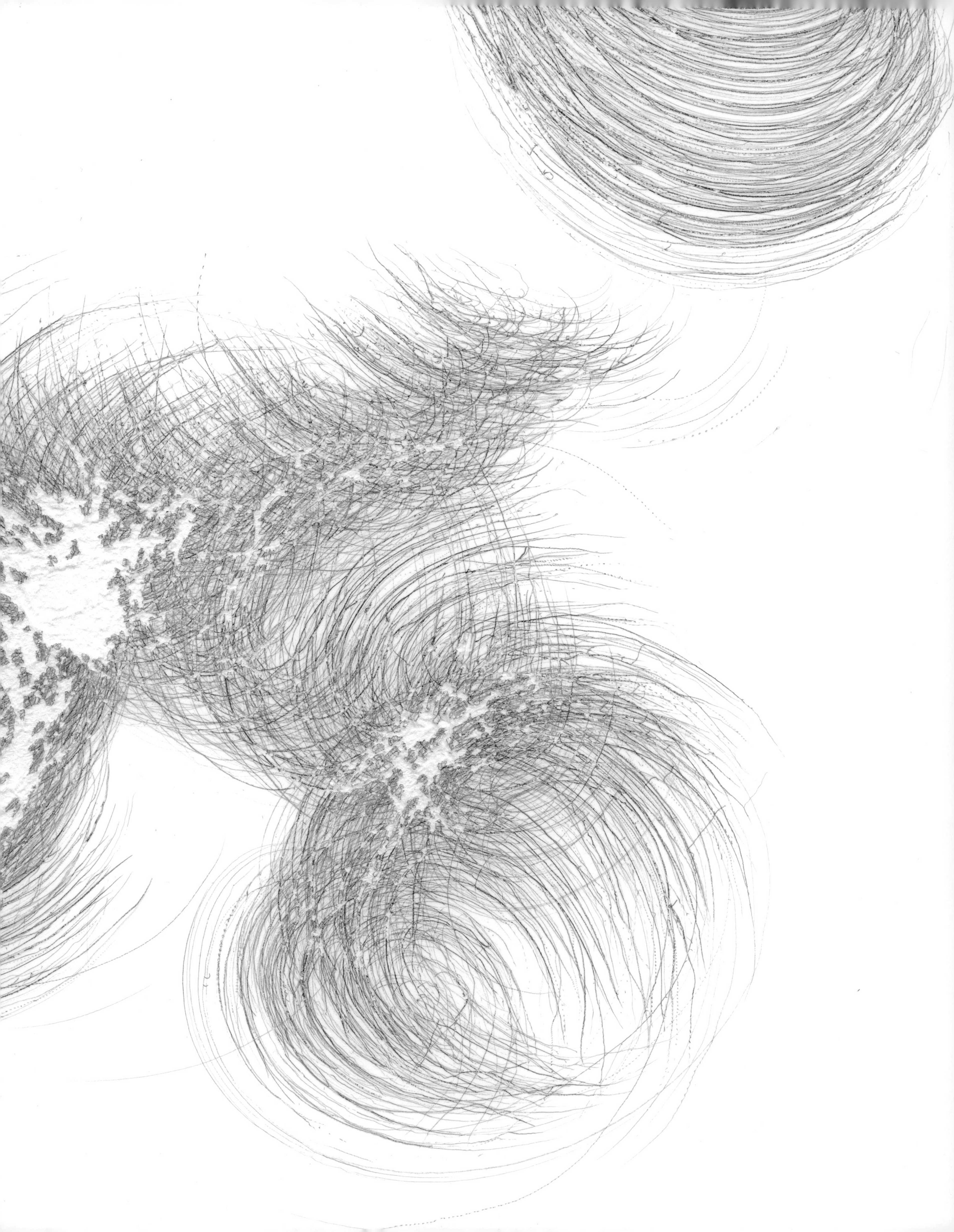

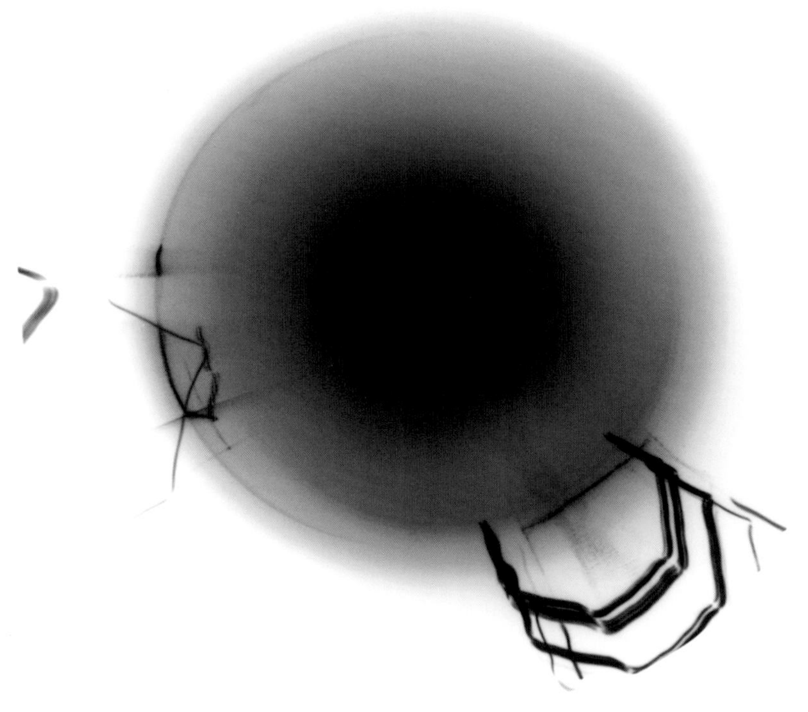

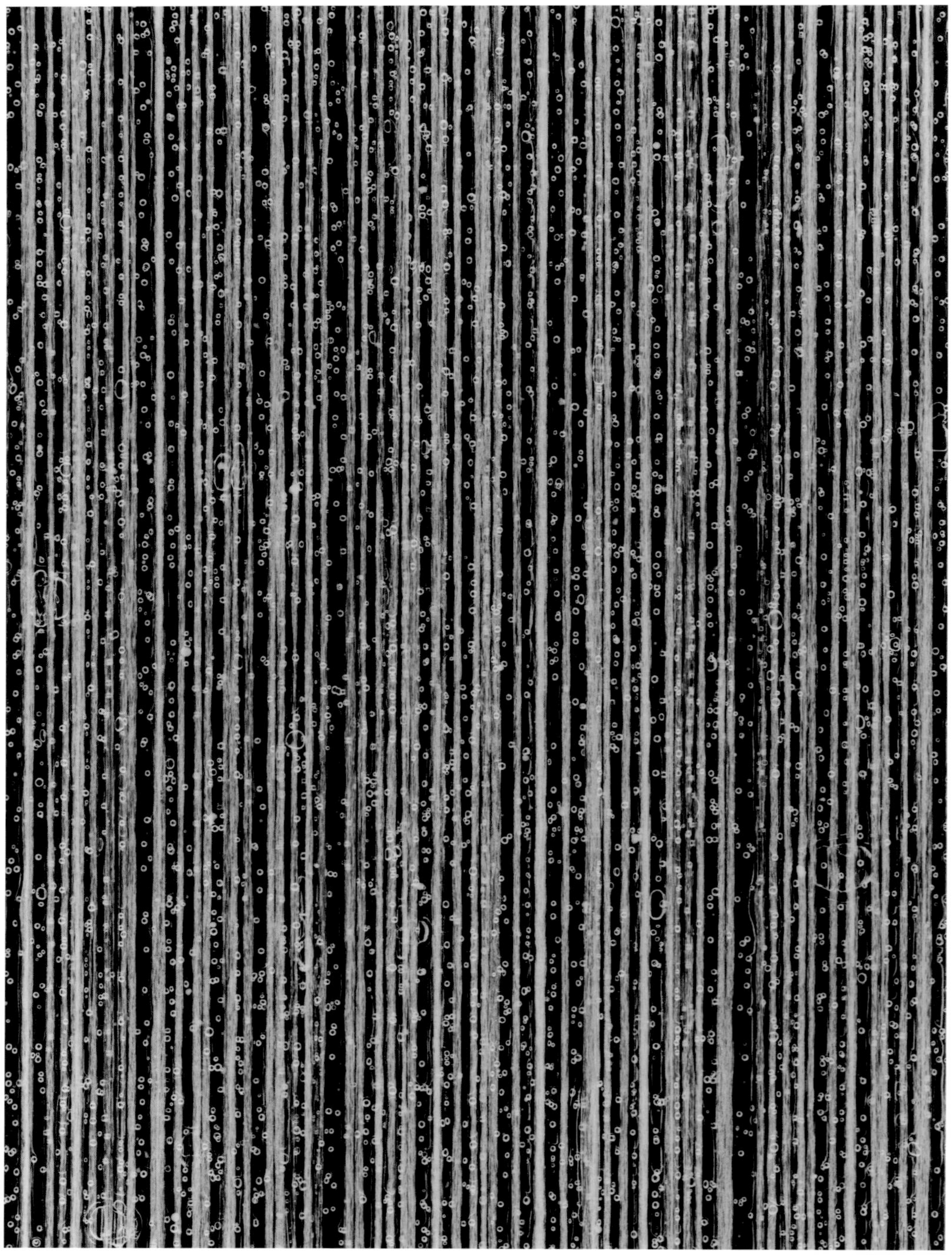

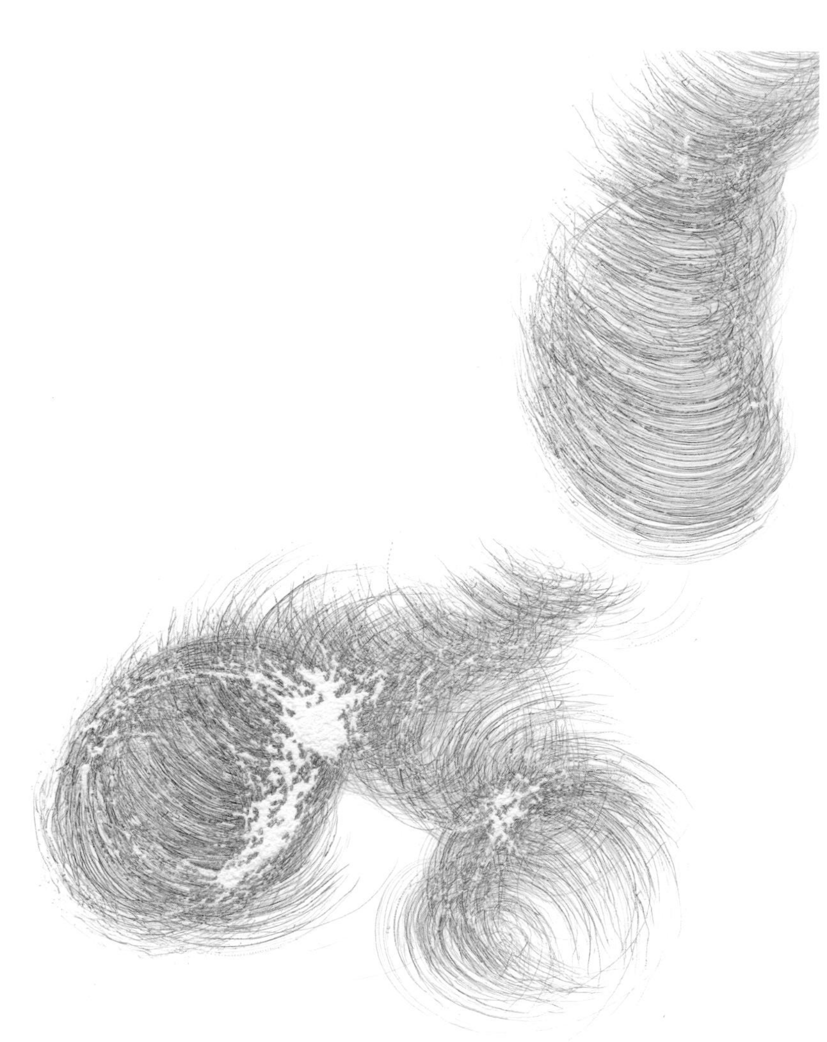

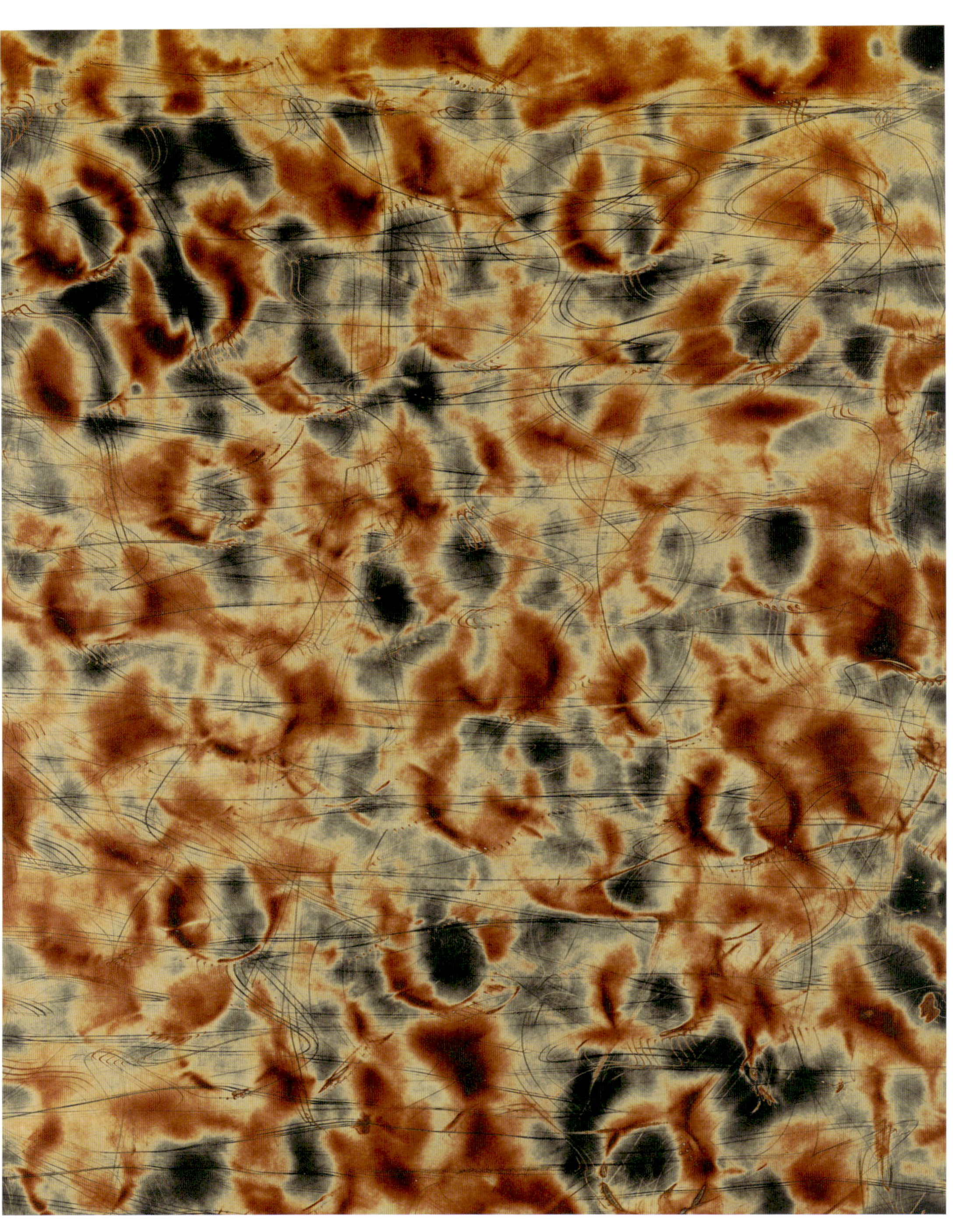

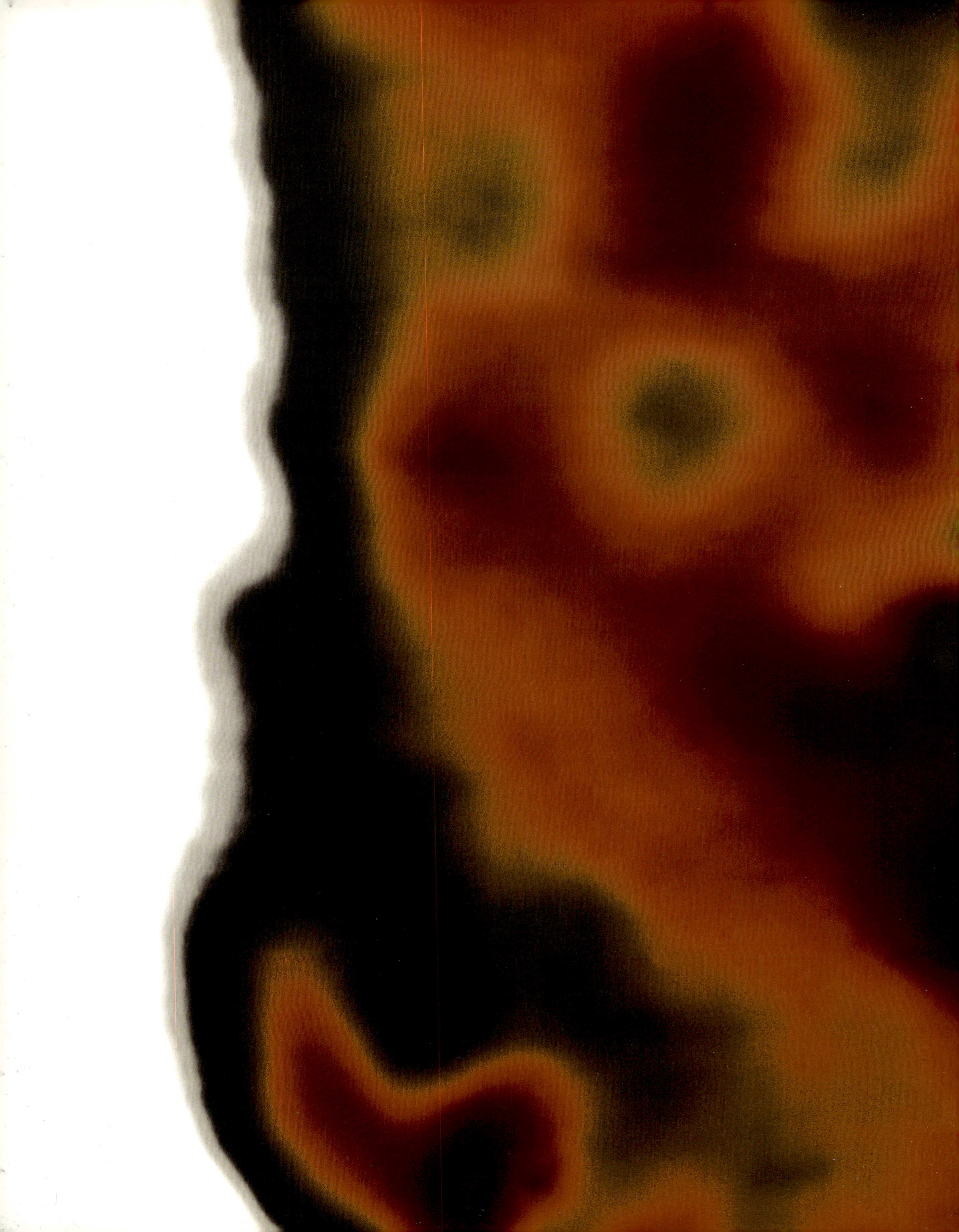

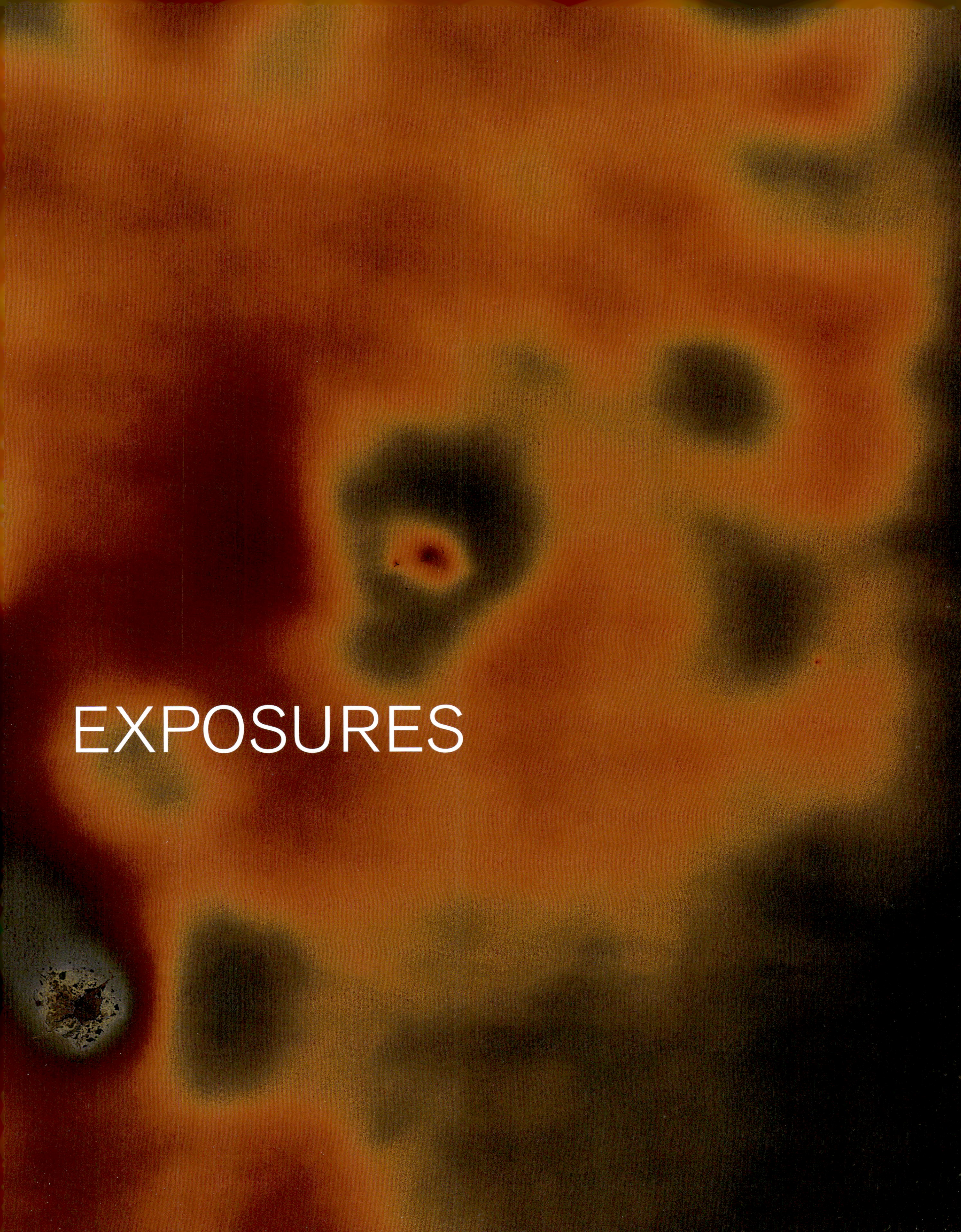
EXPOSURES

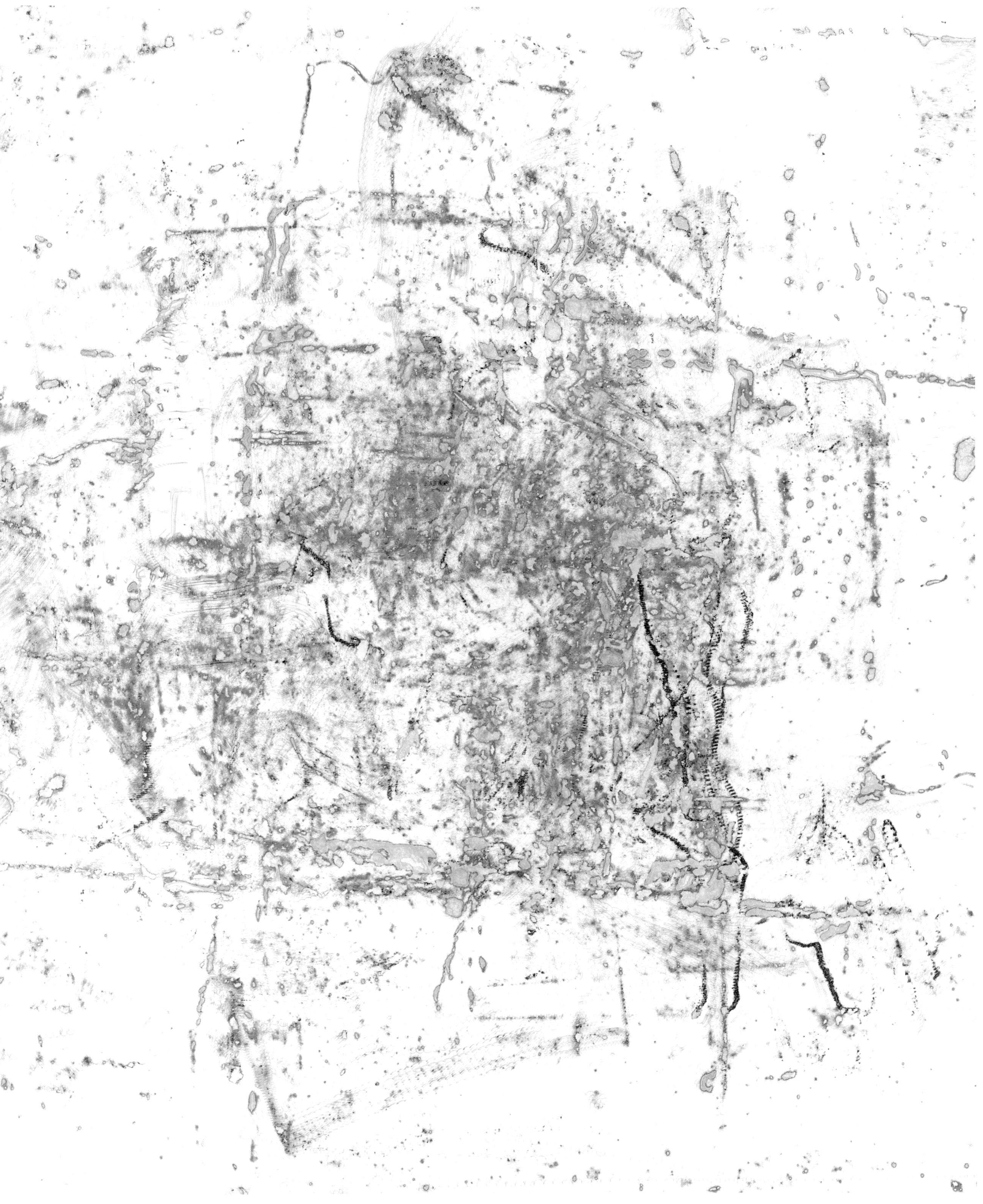

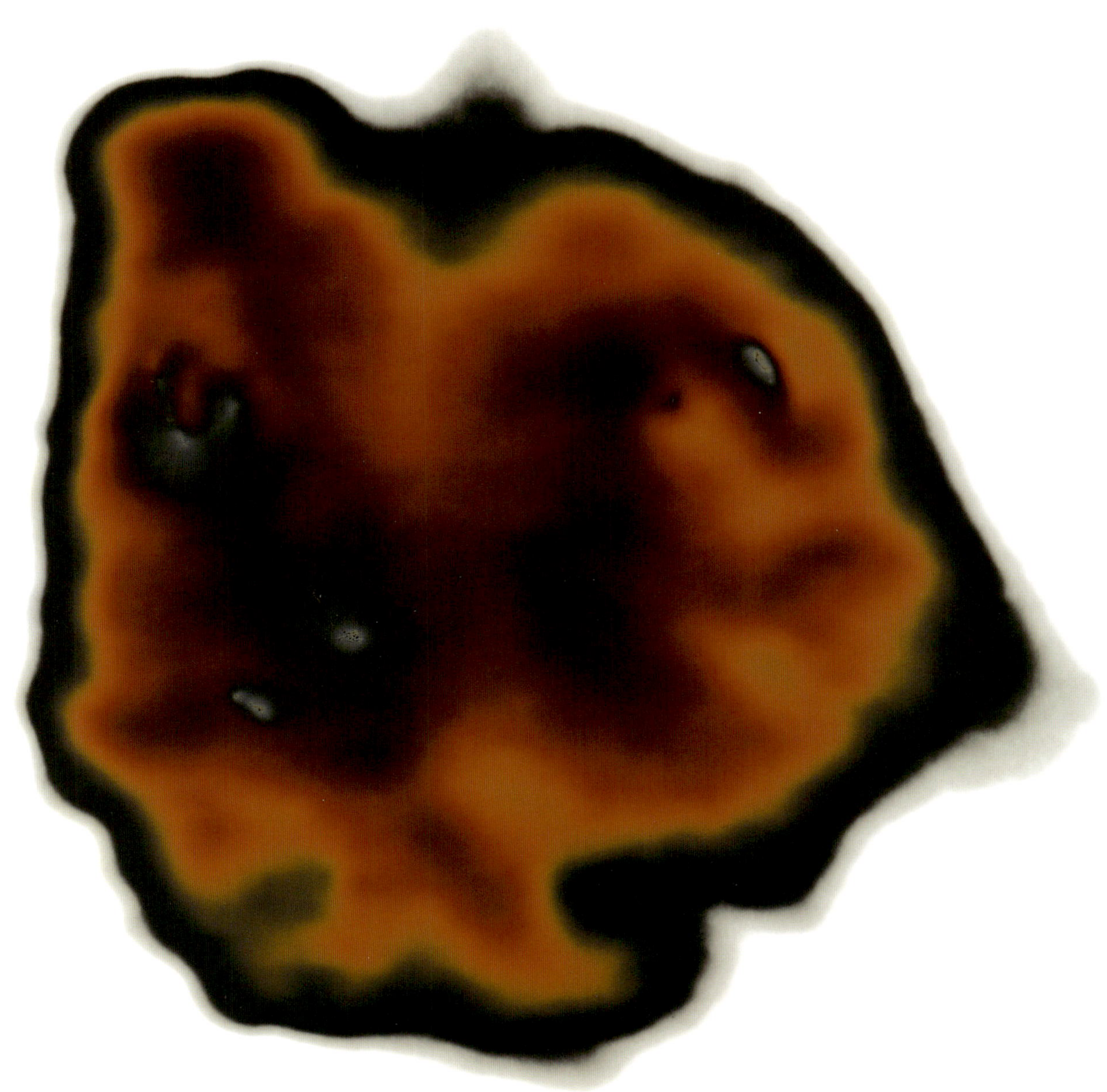

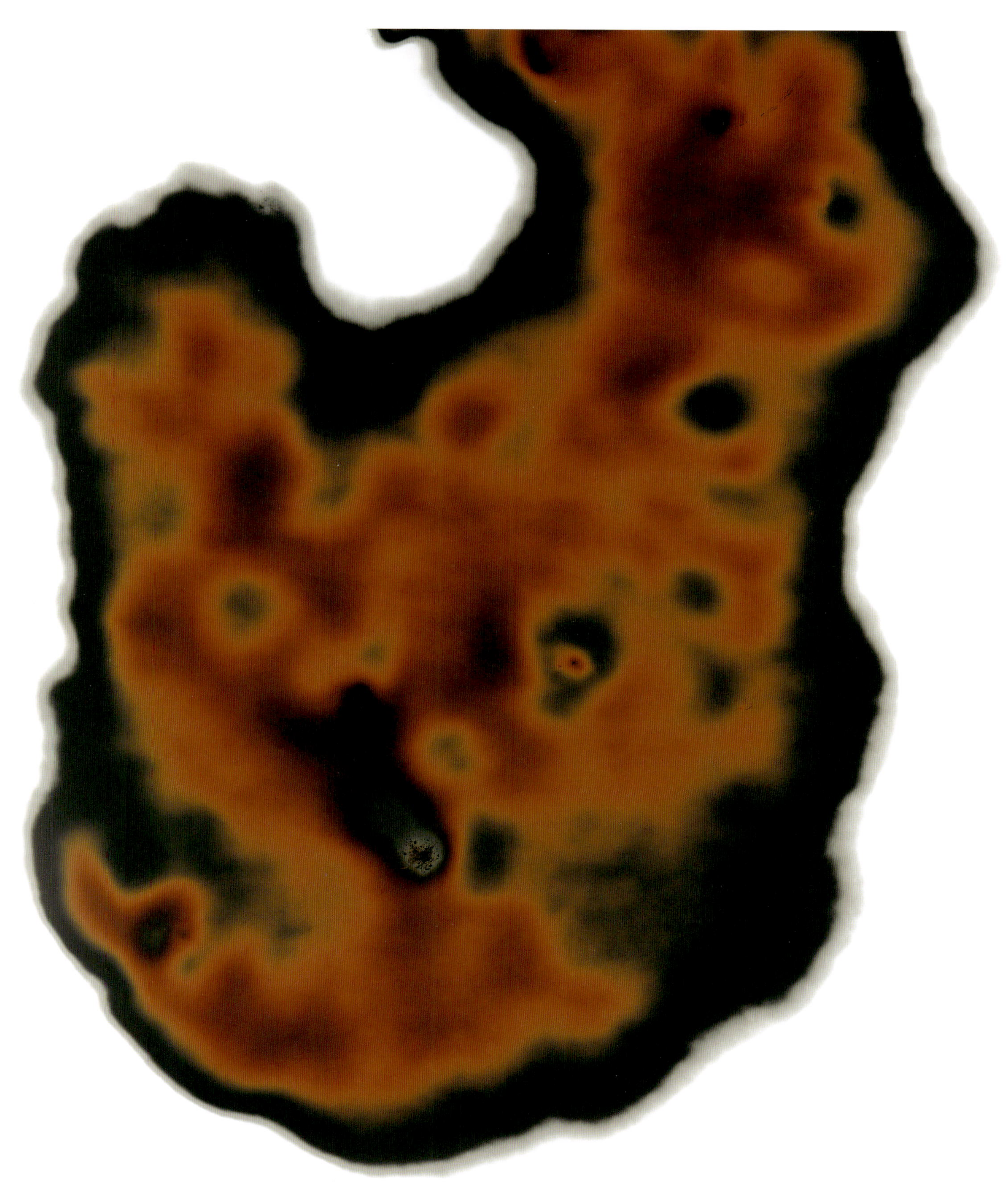

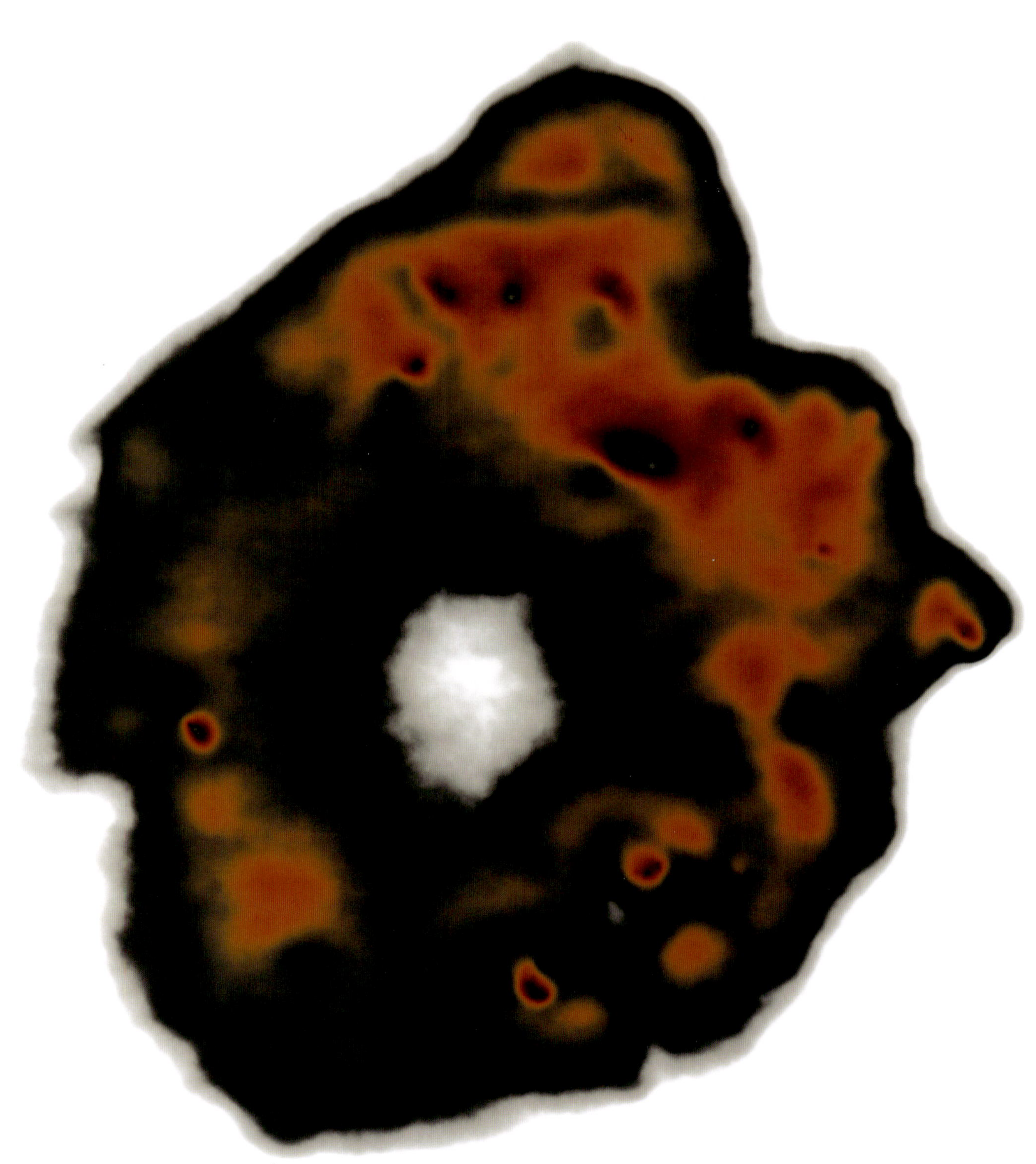

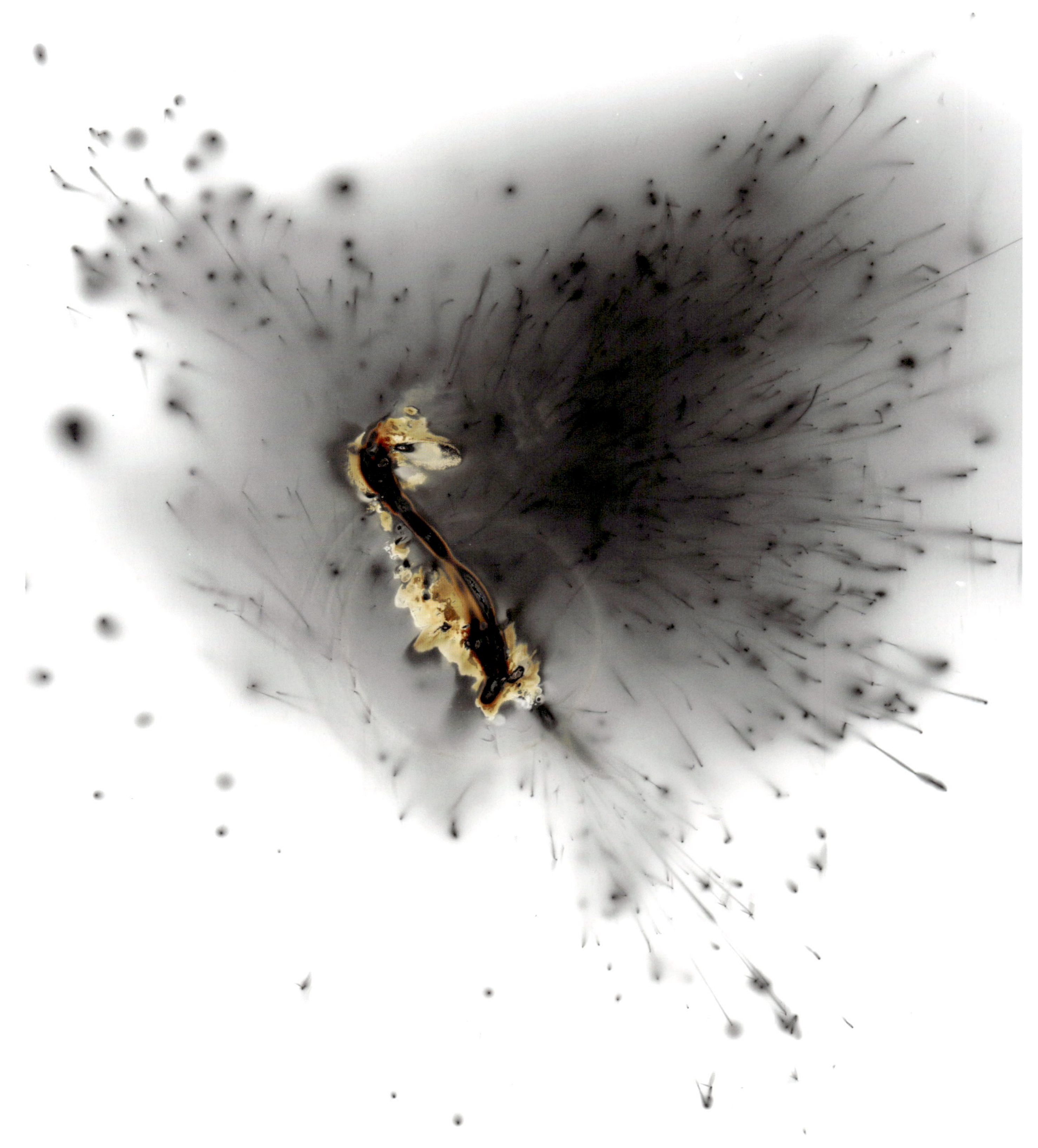

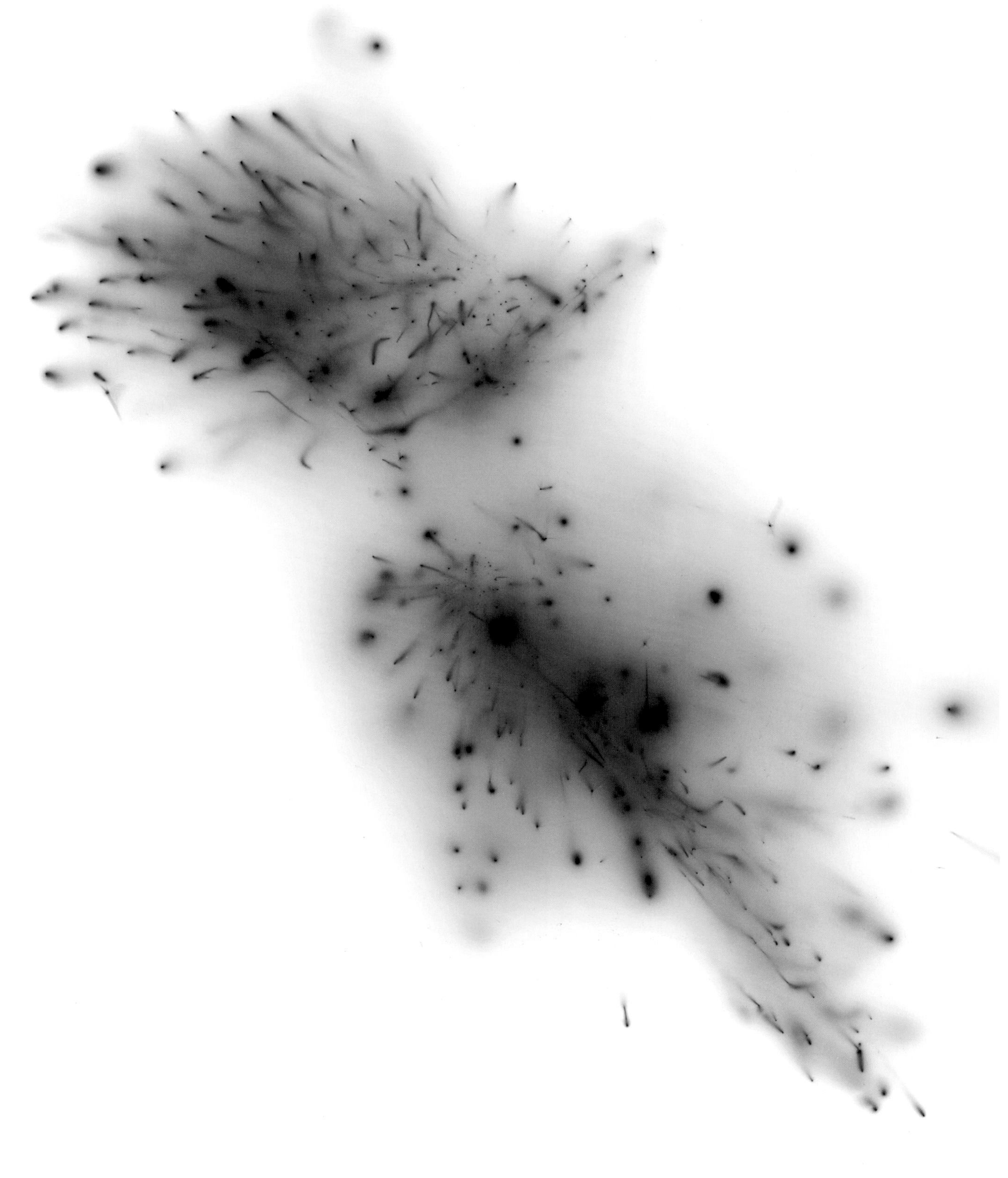

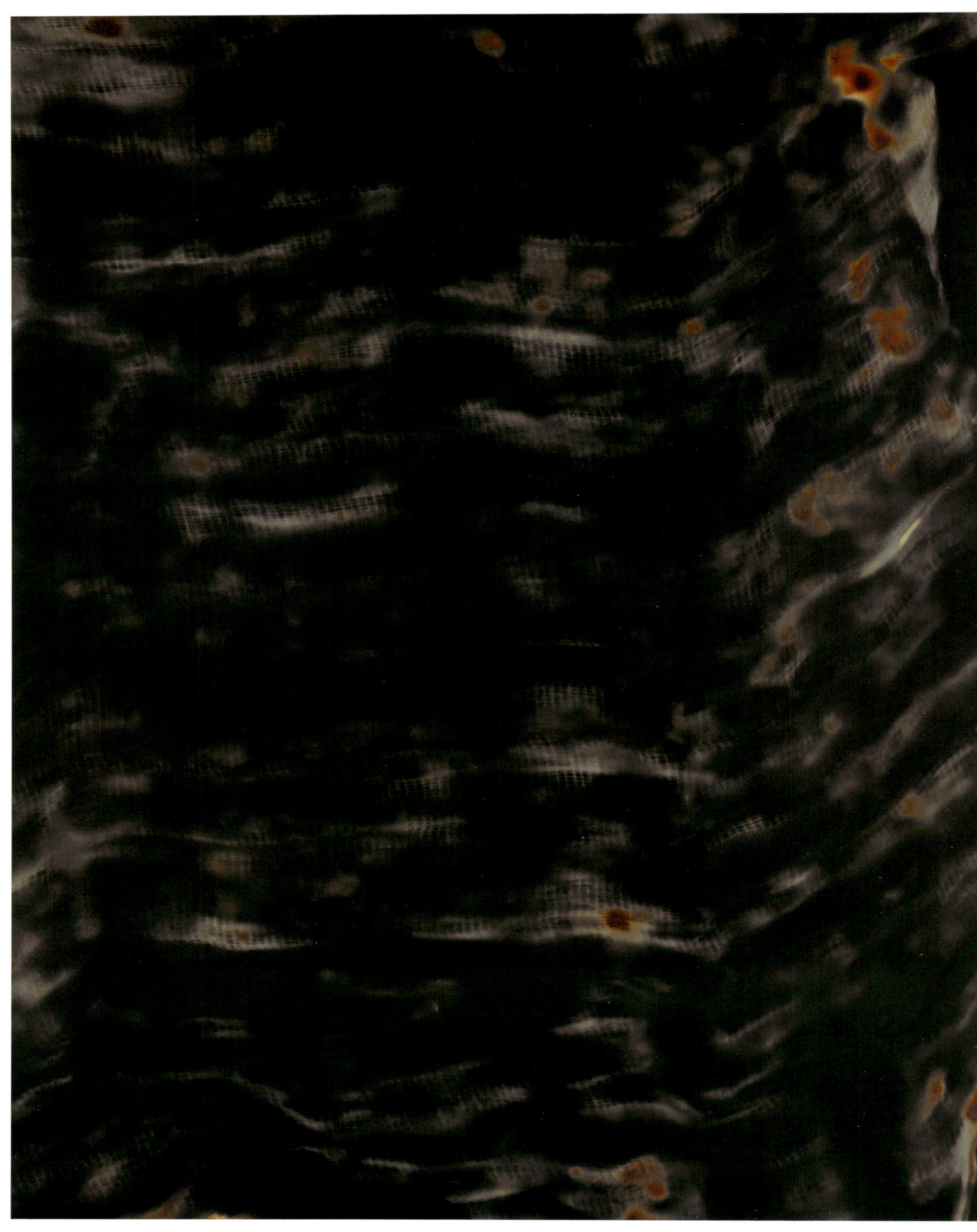

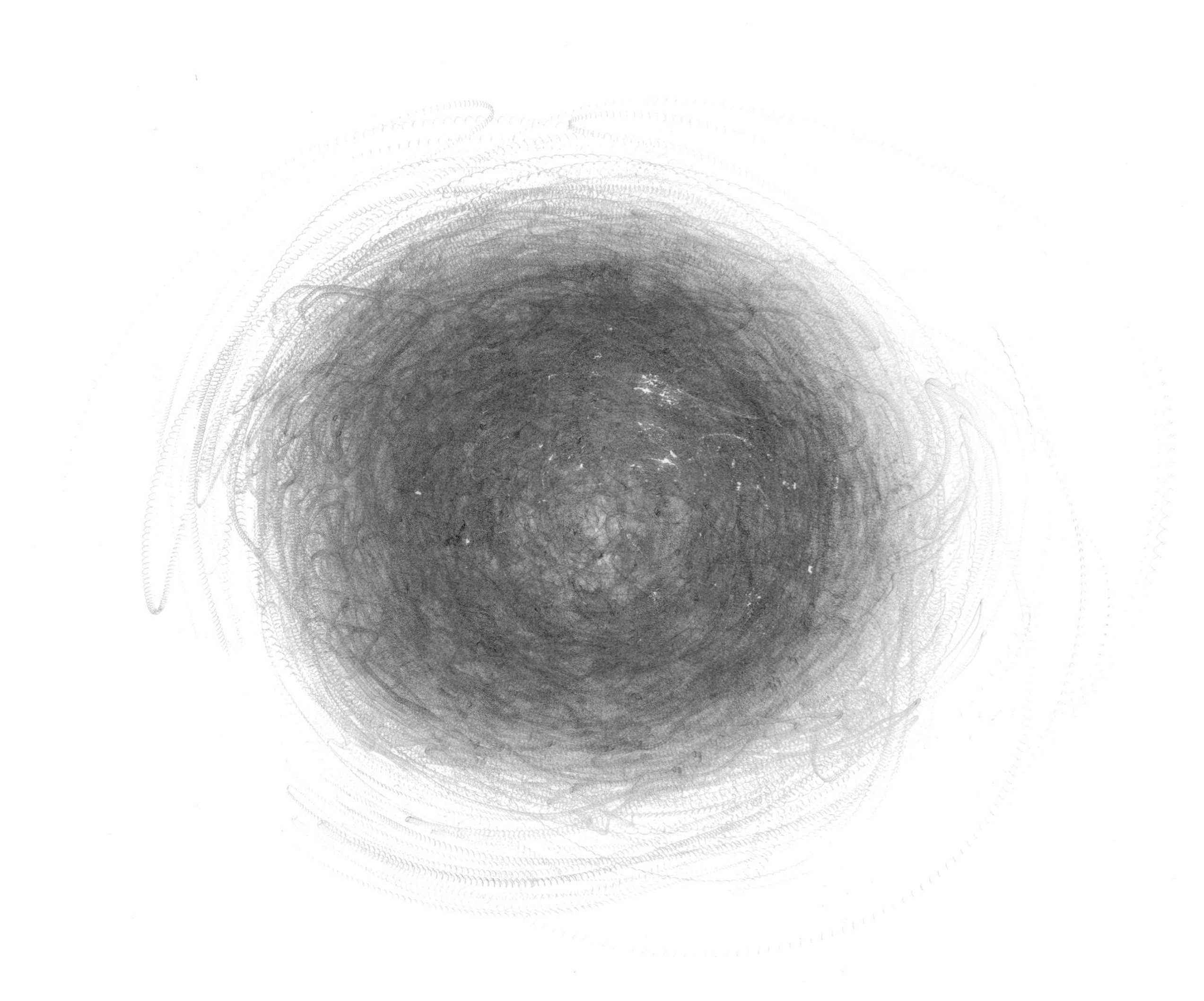

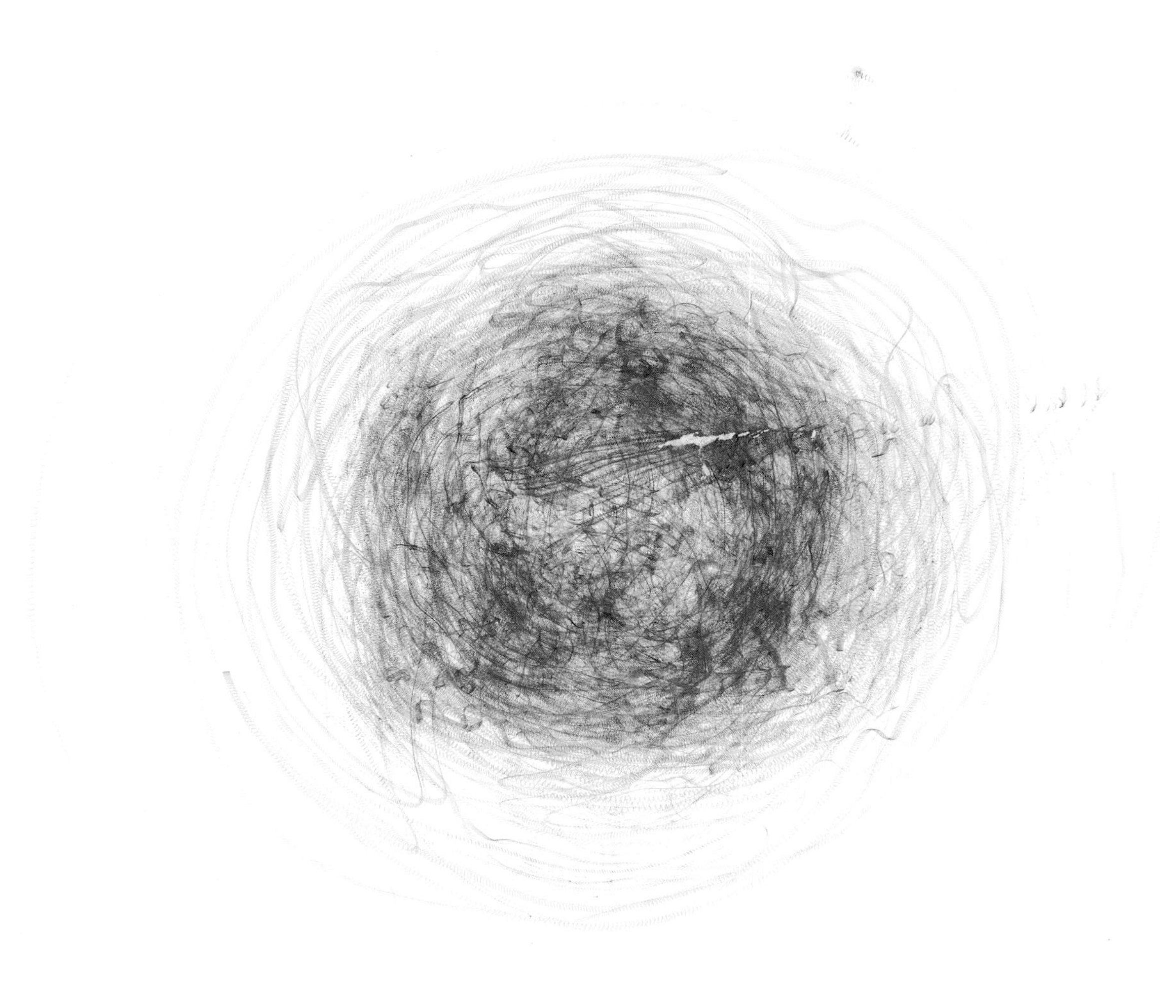

PAN AND TILT

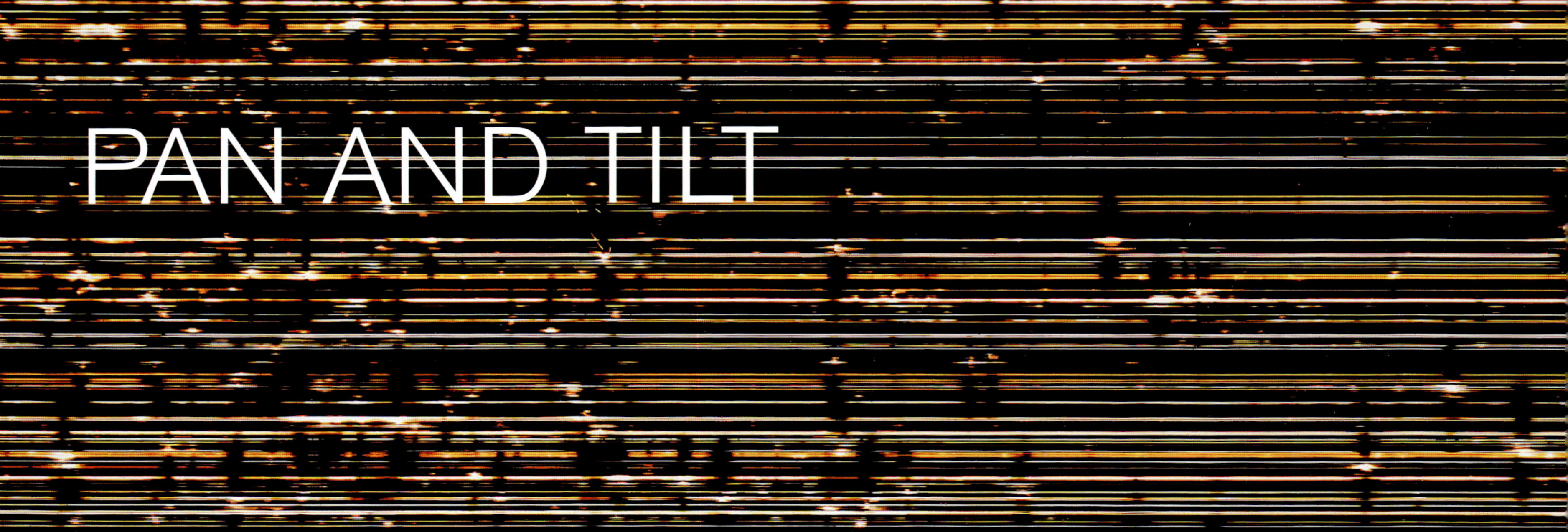

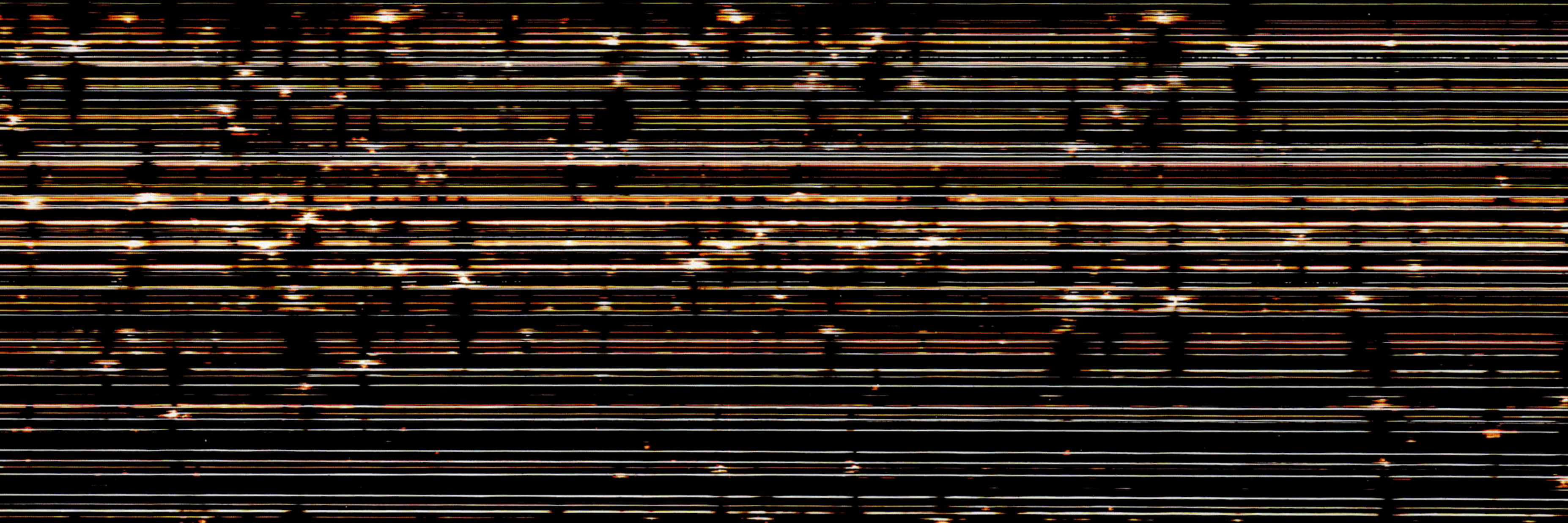

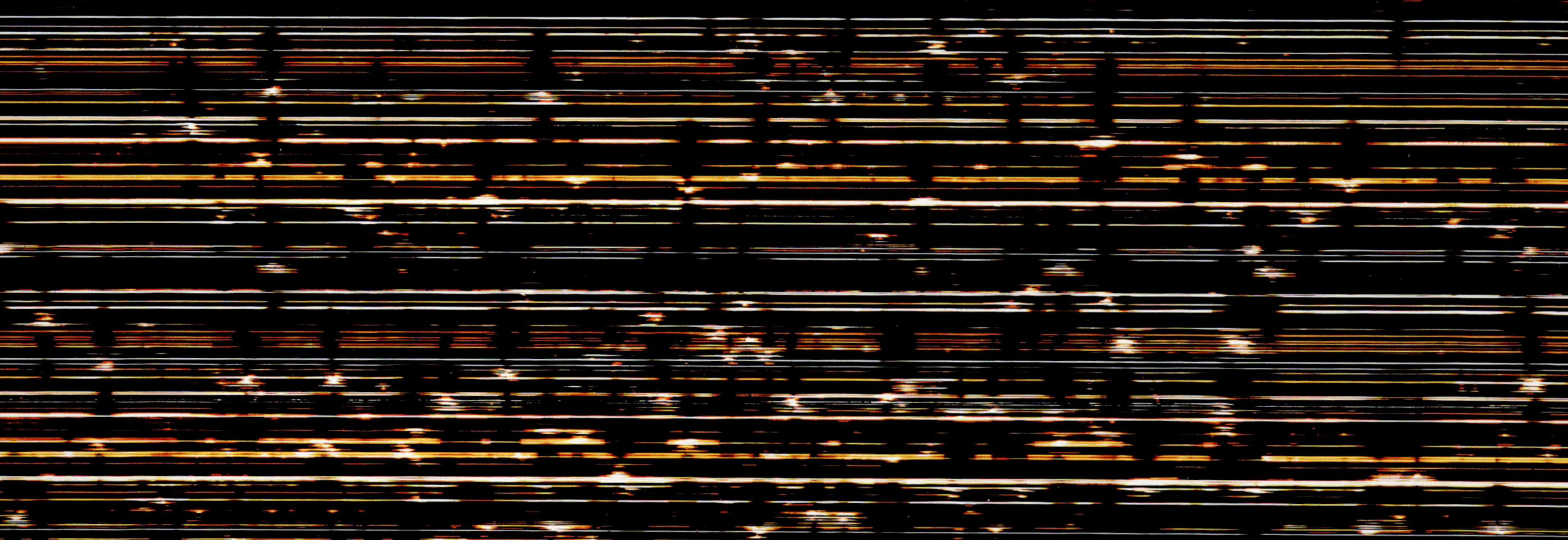

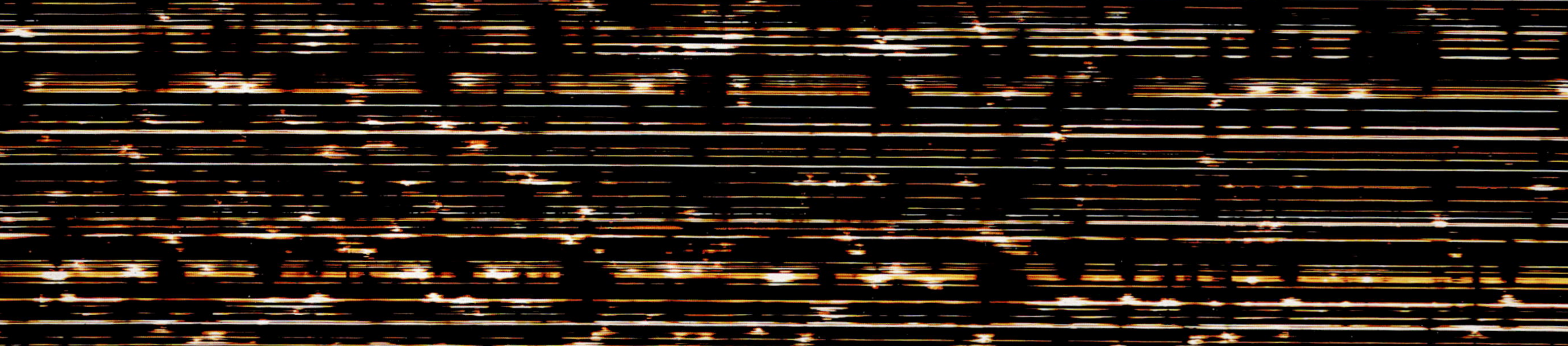

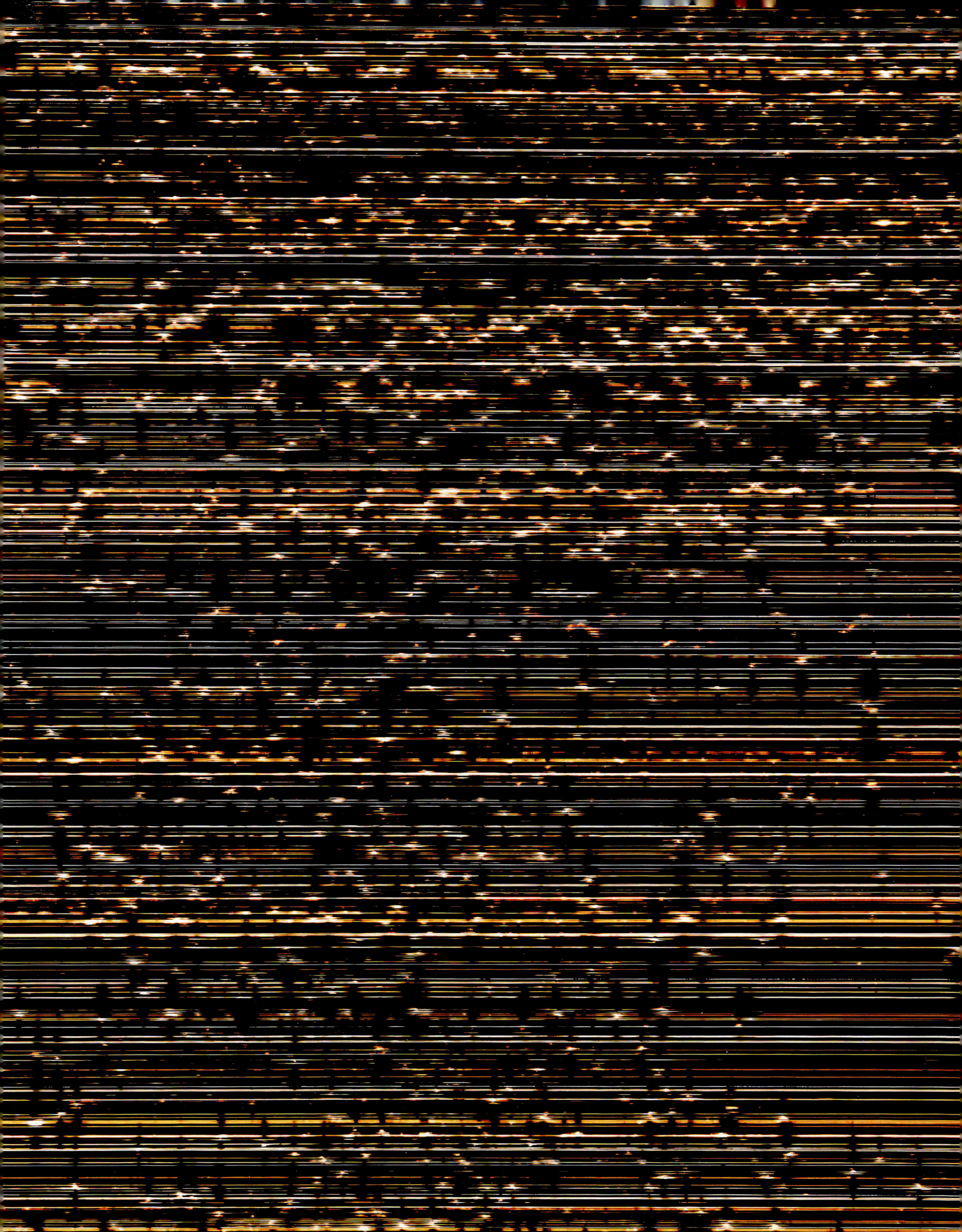

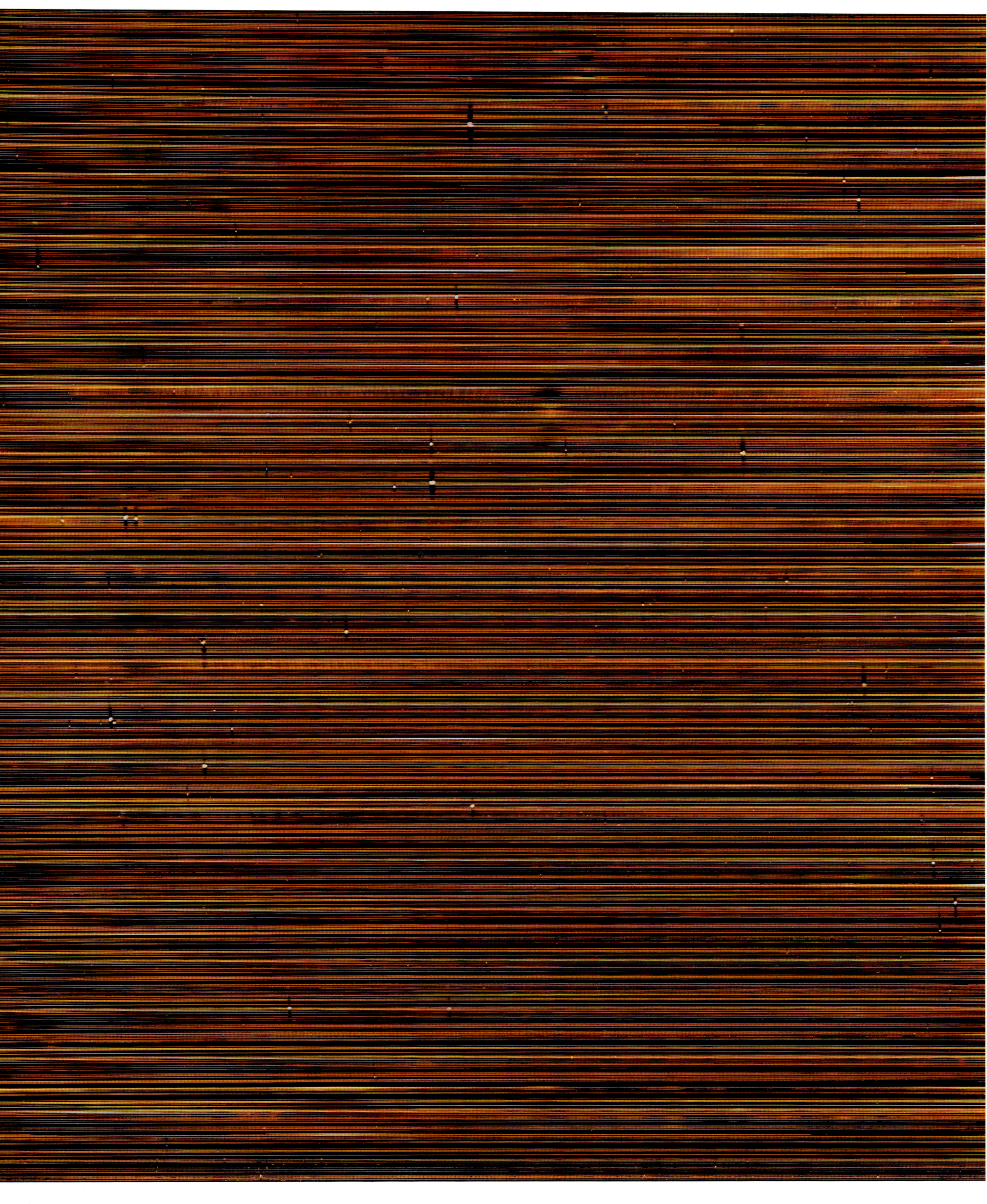

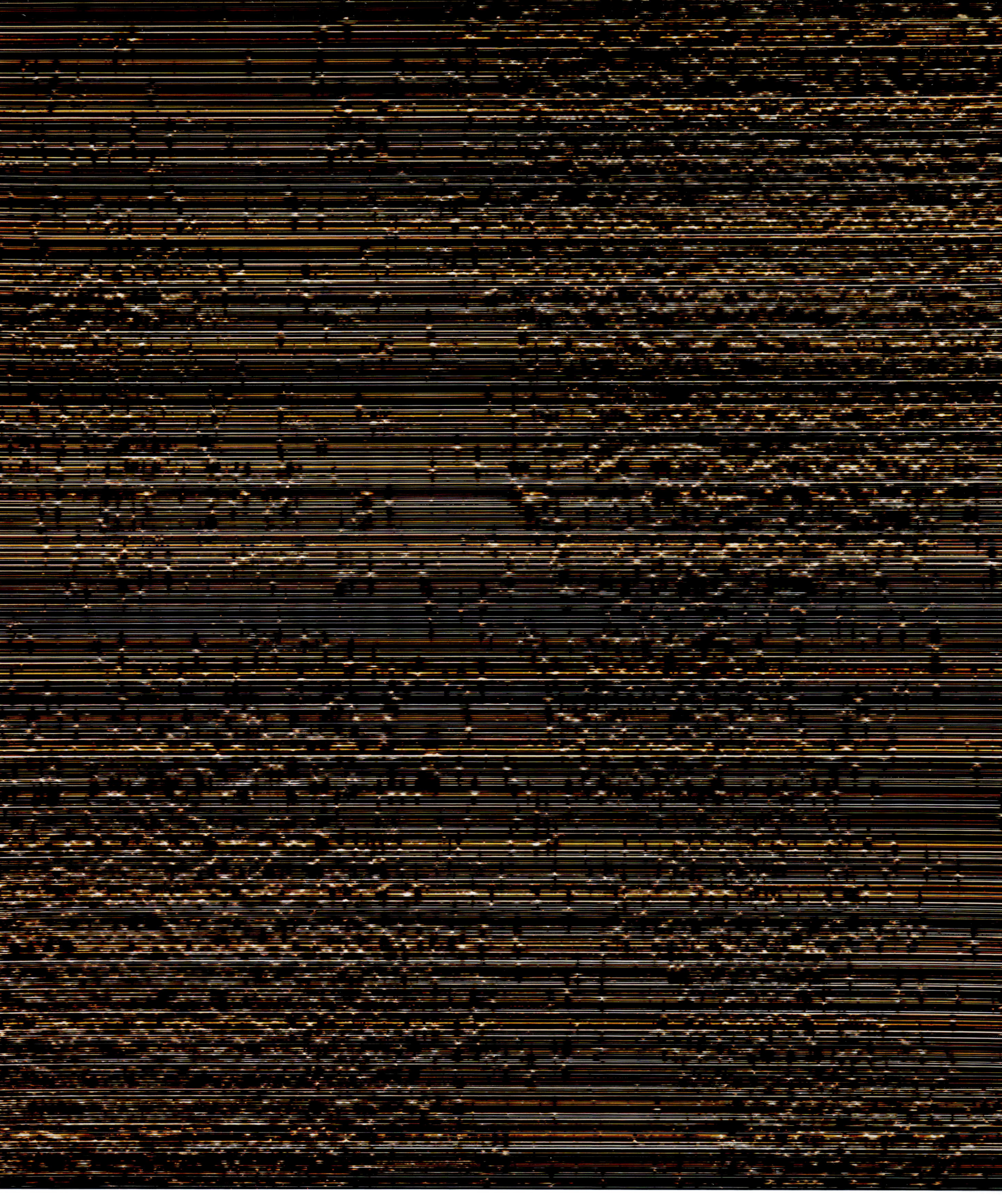

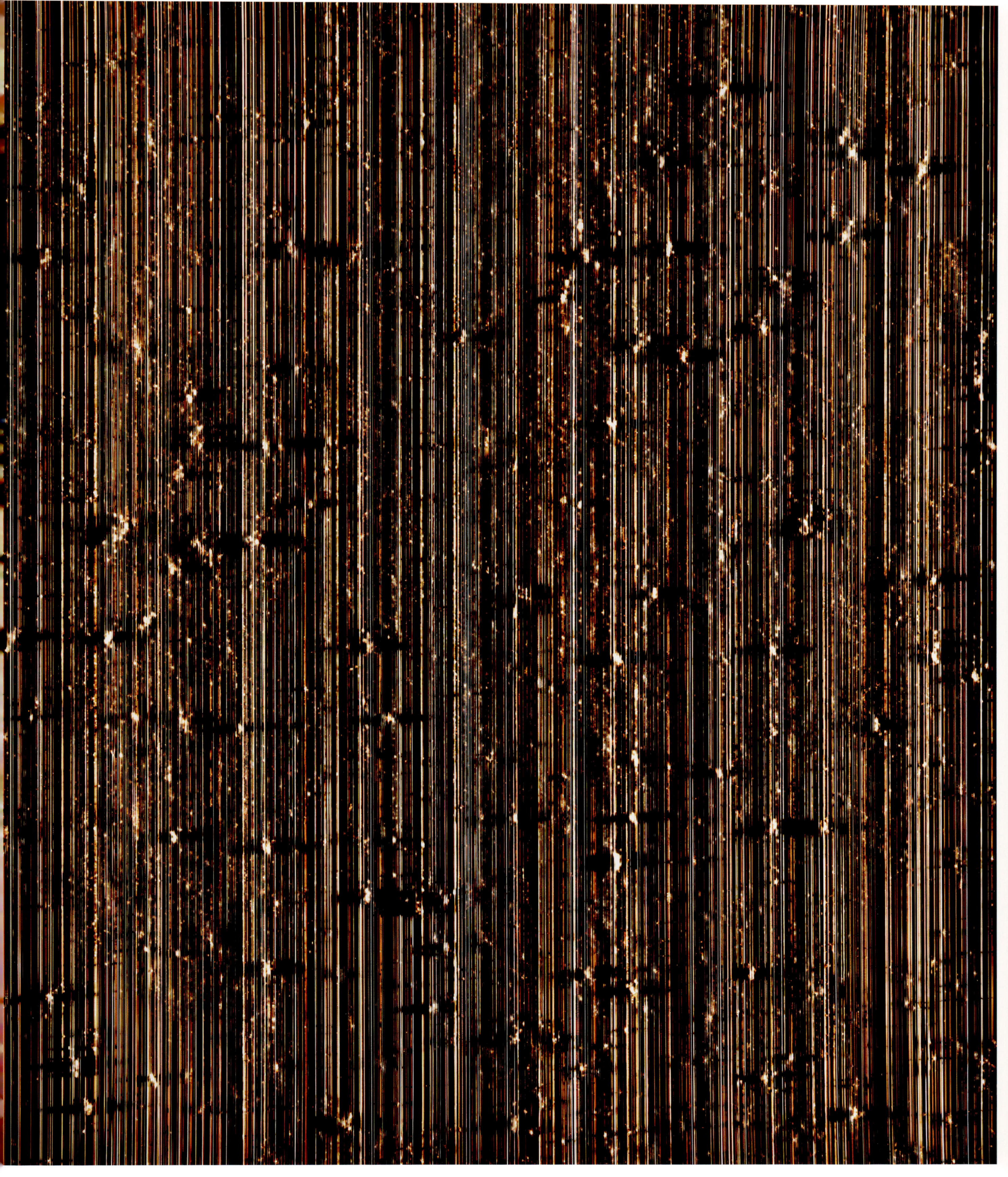

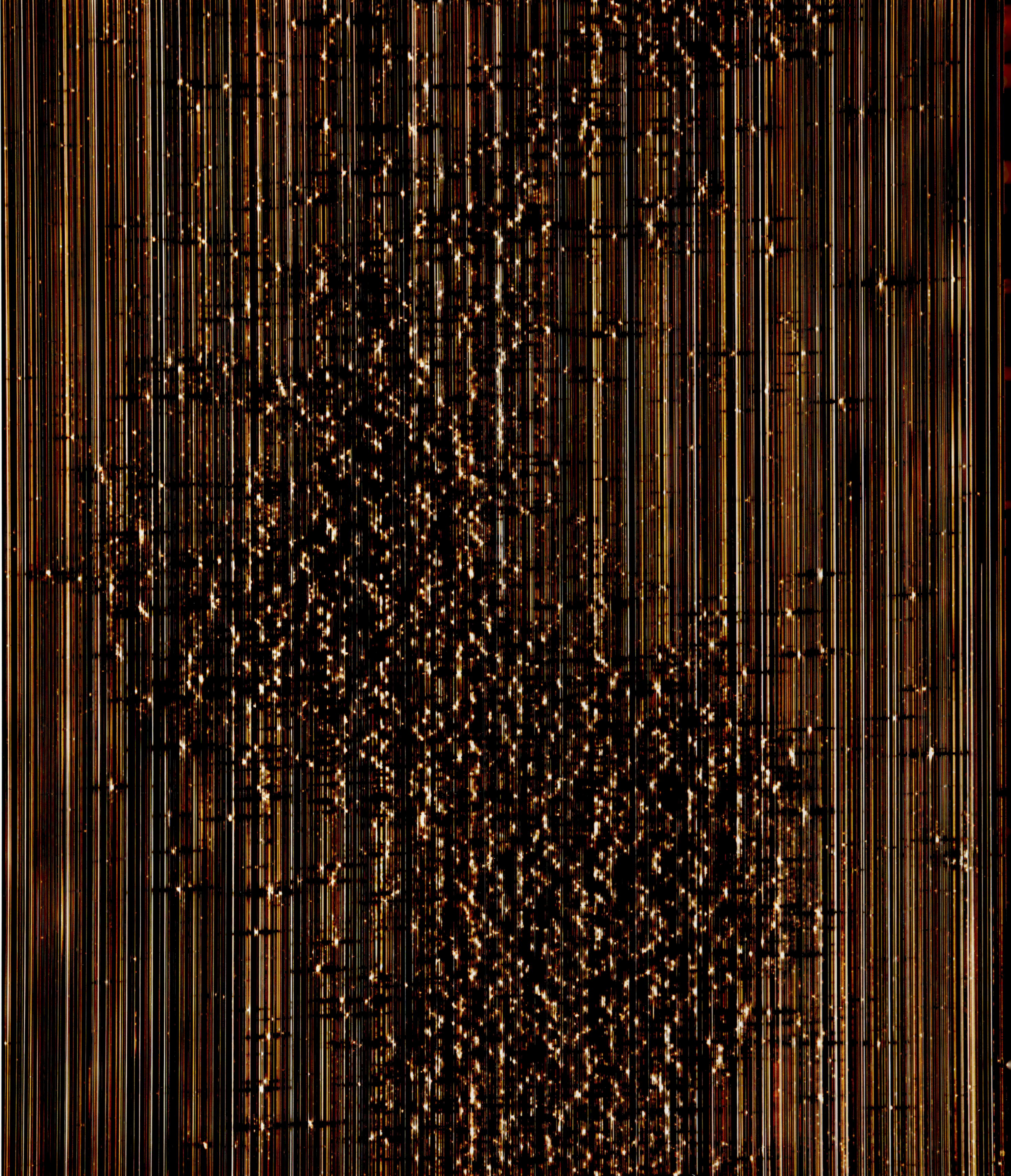

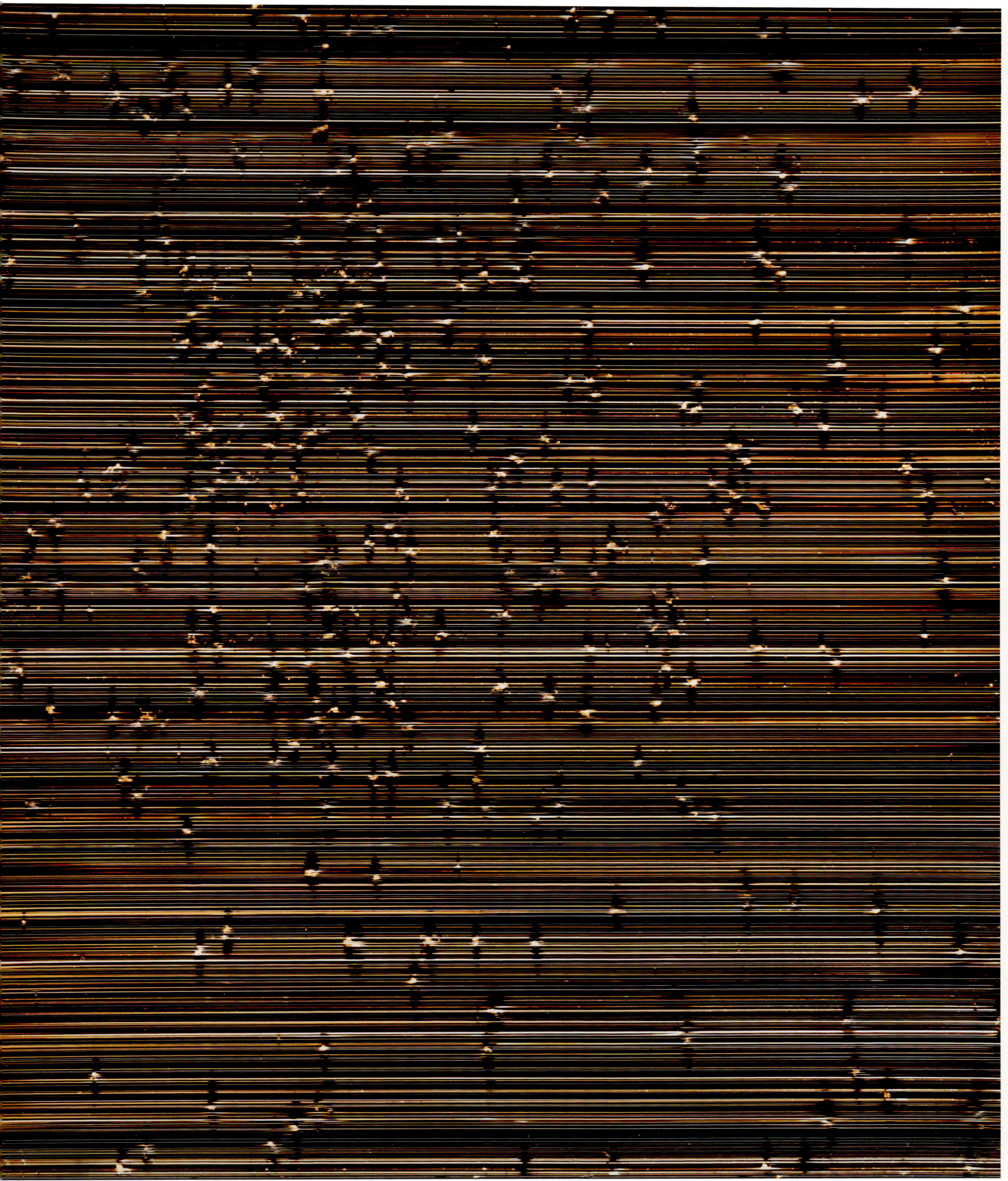

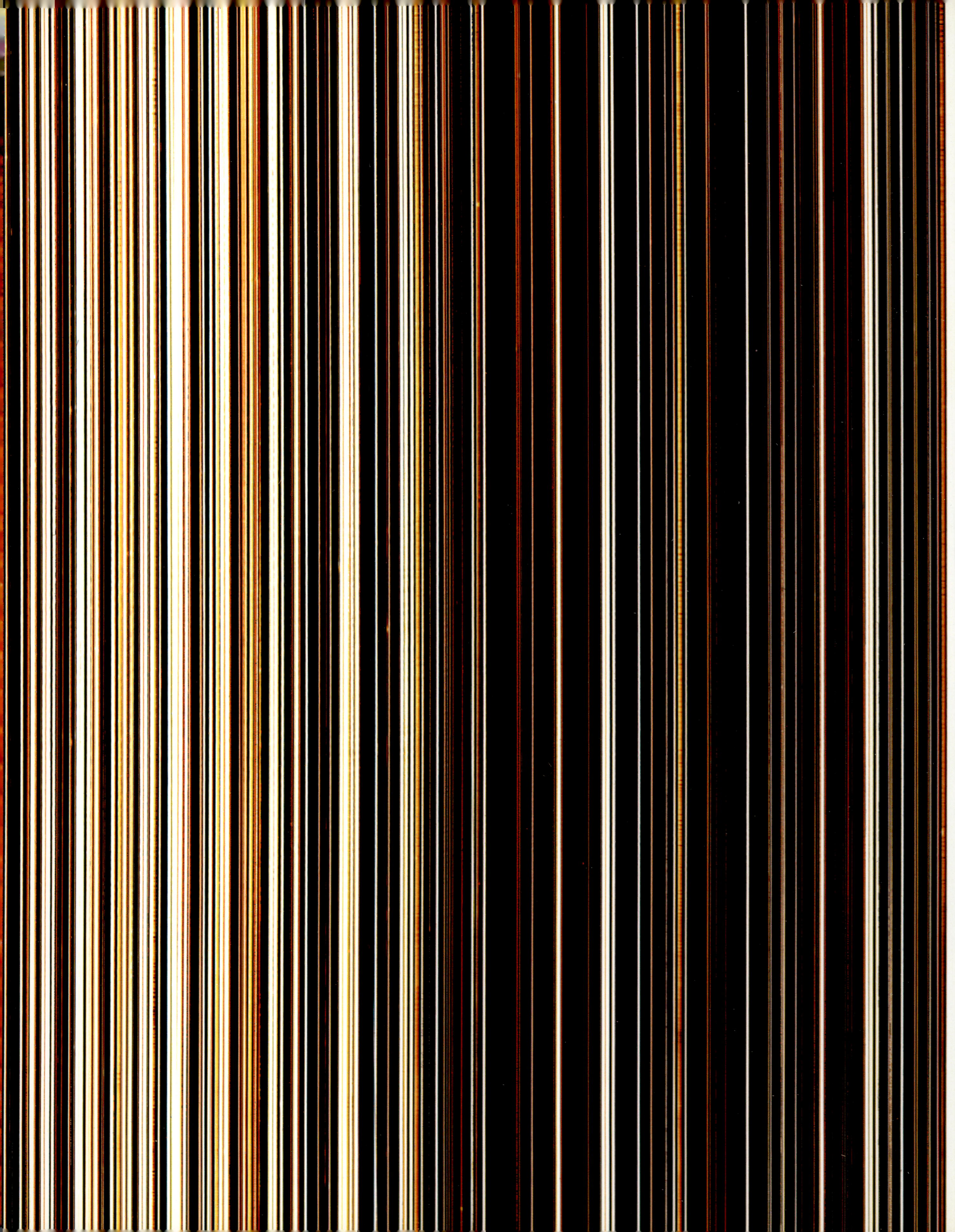

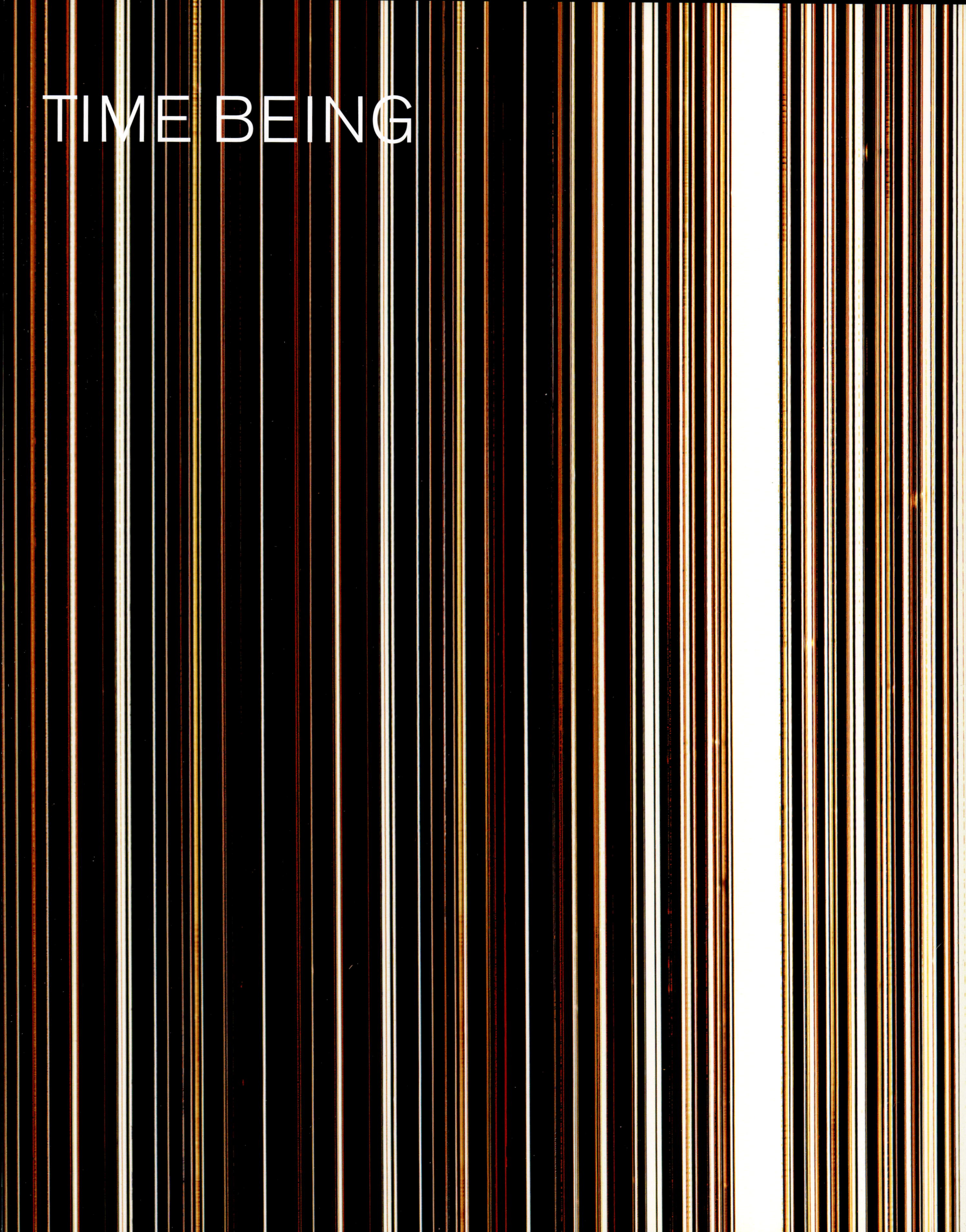
TIME BEING

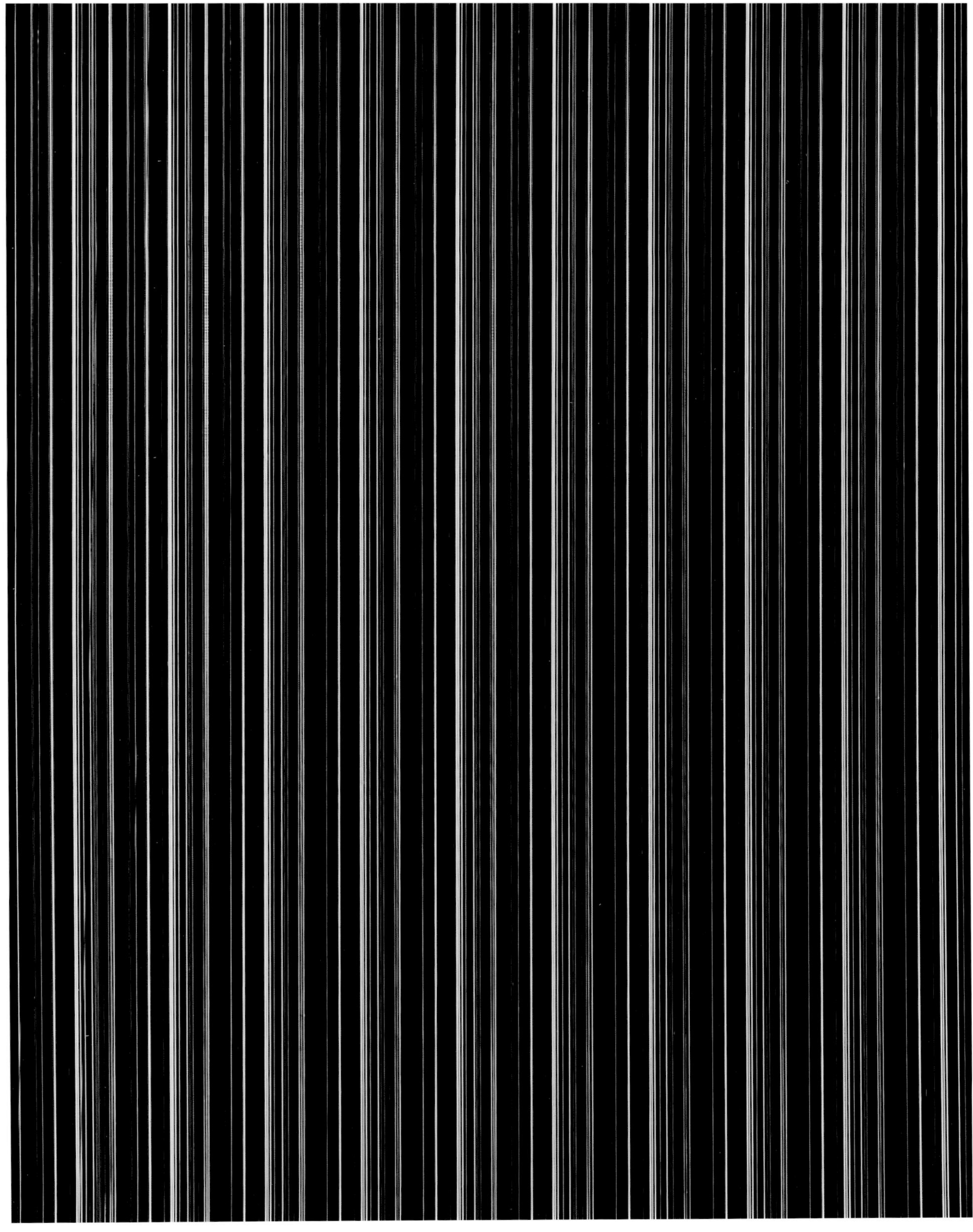

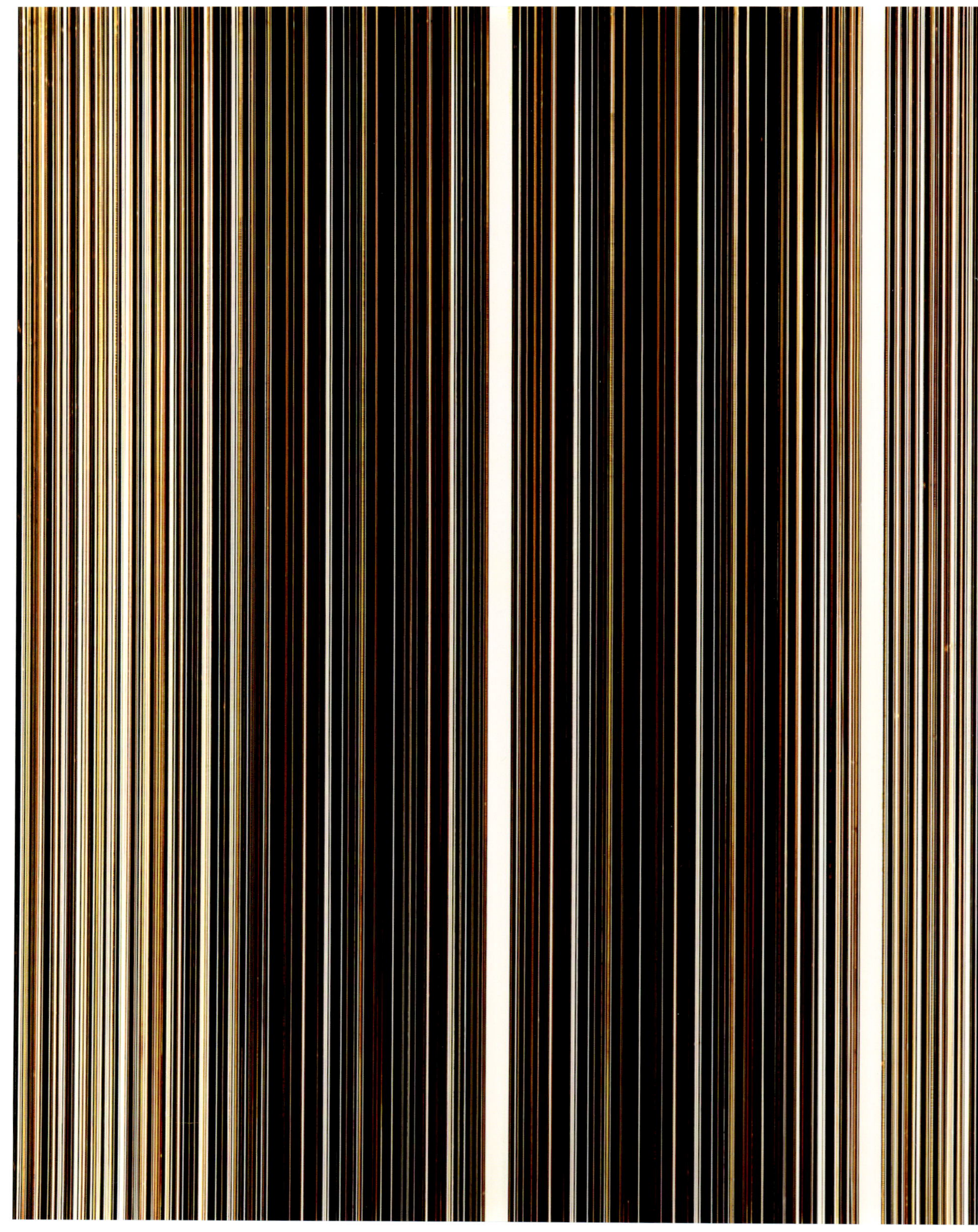

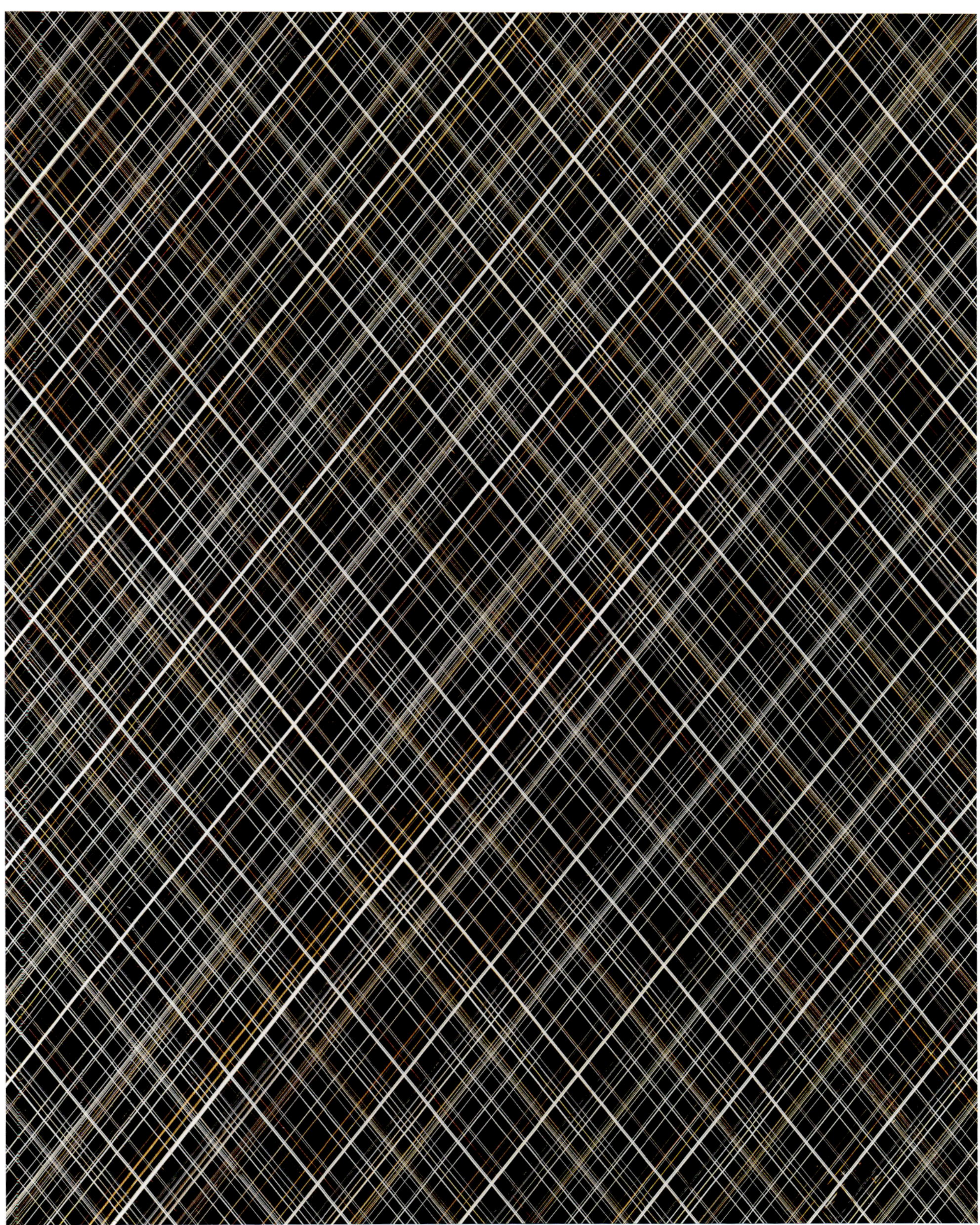

COMPLICATIONS (PROBLEM I–IV)

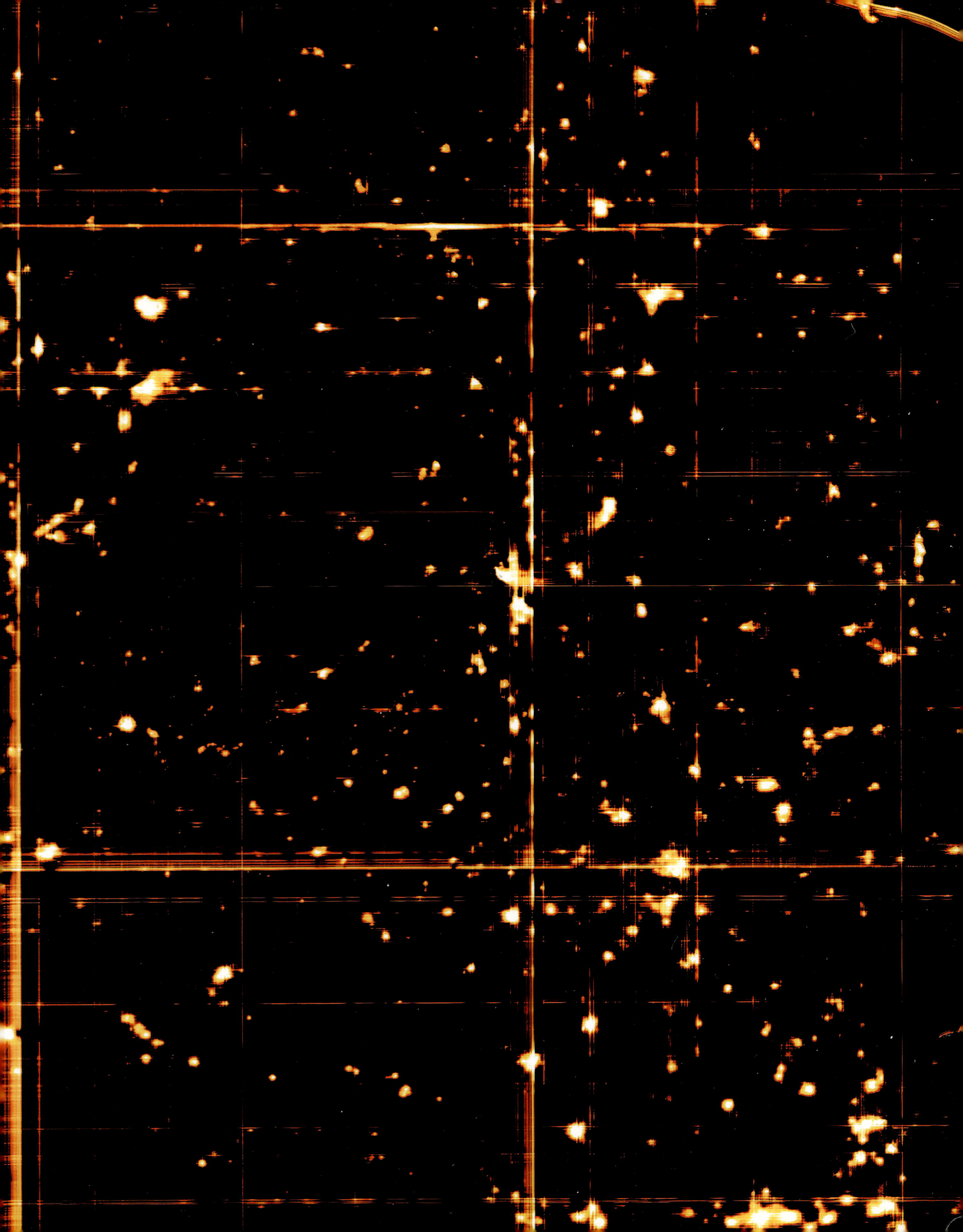

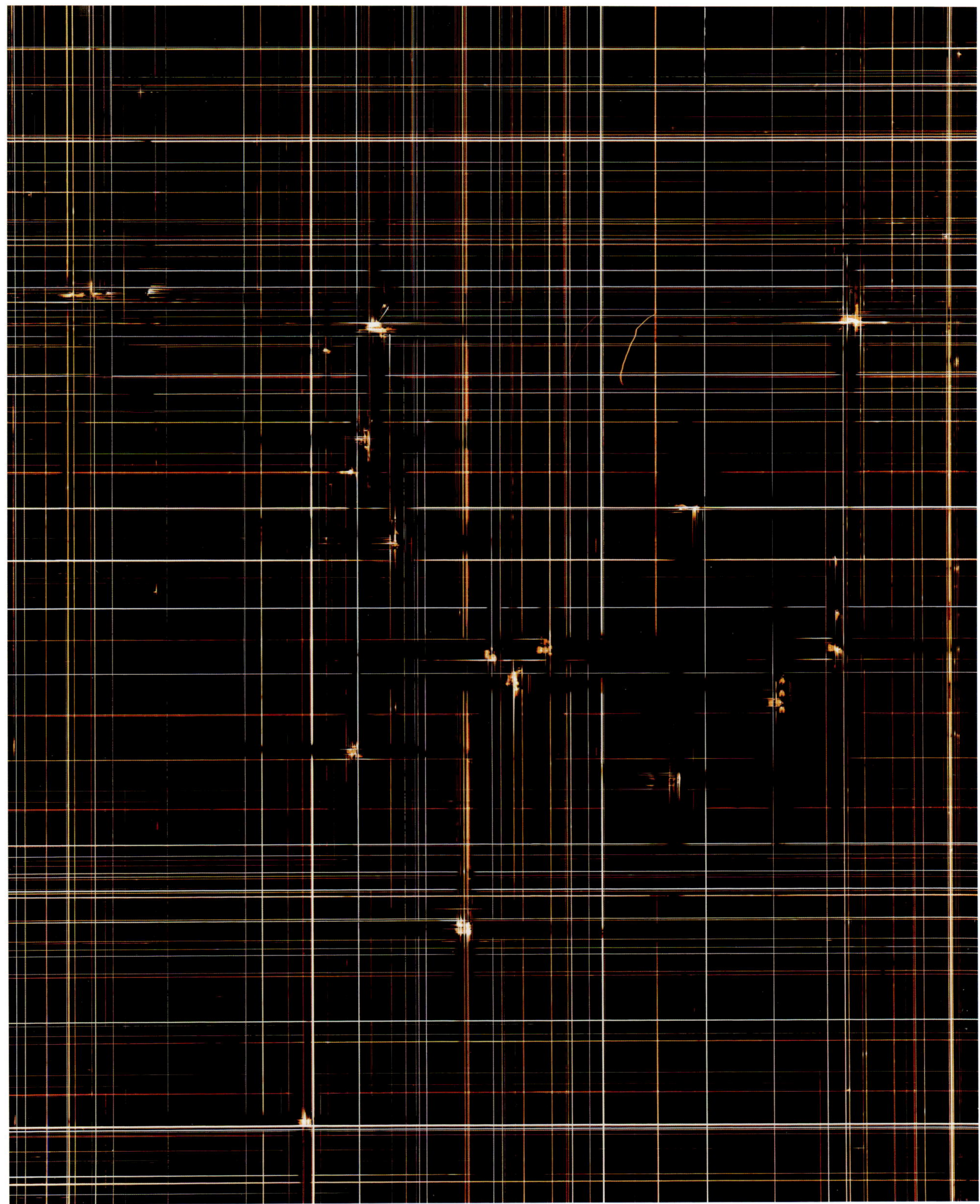

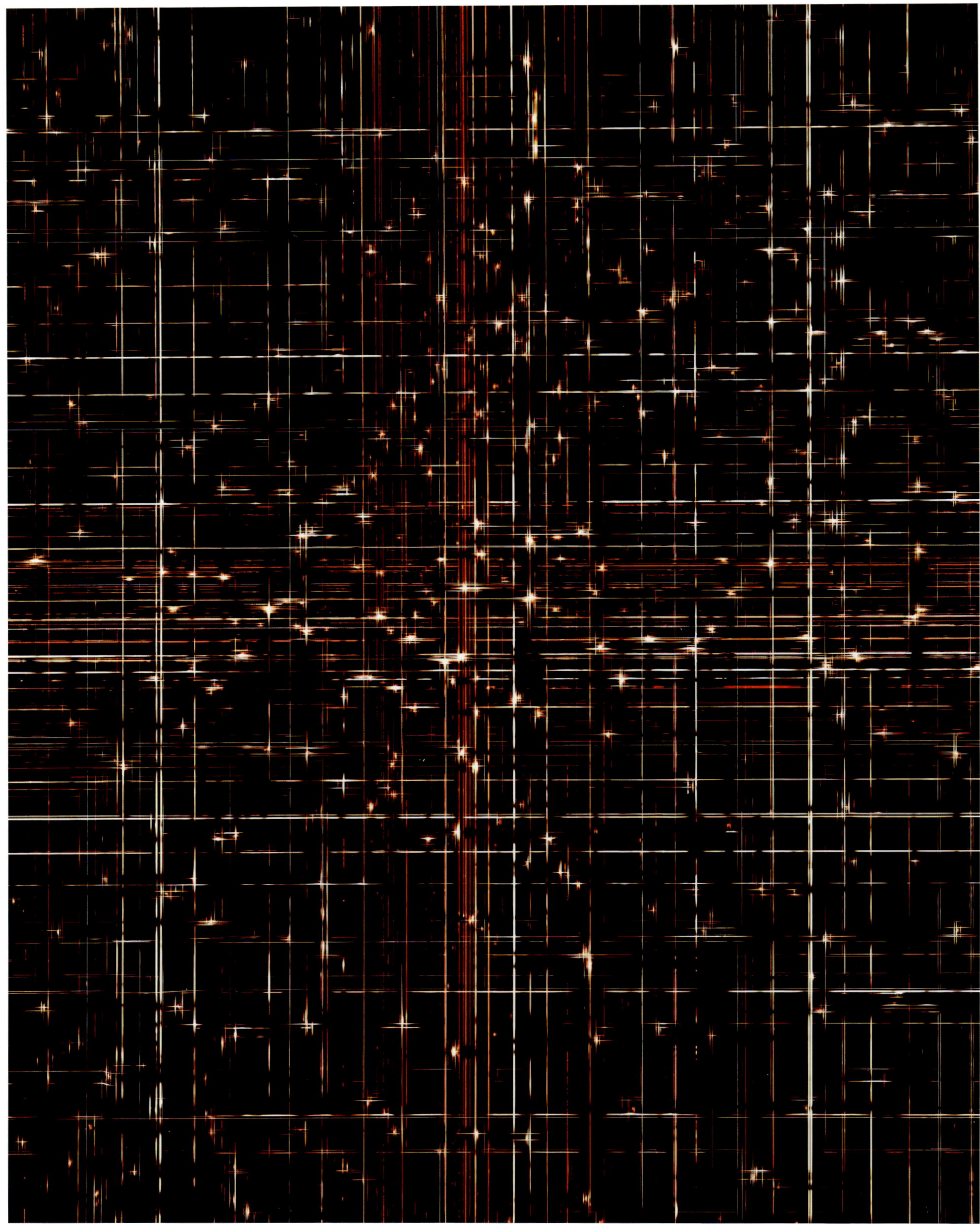

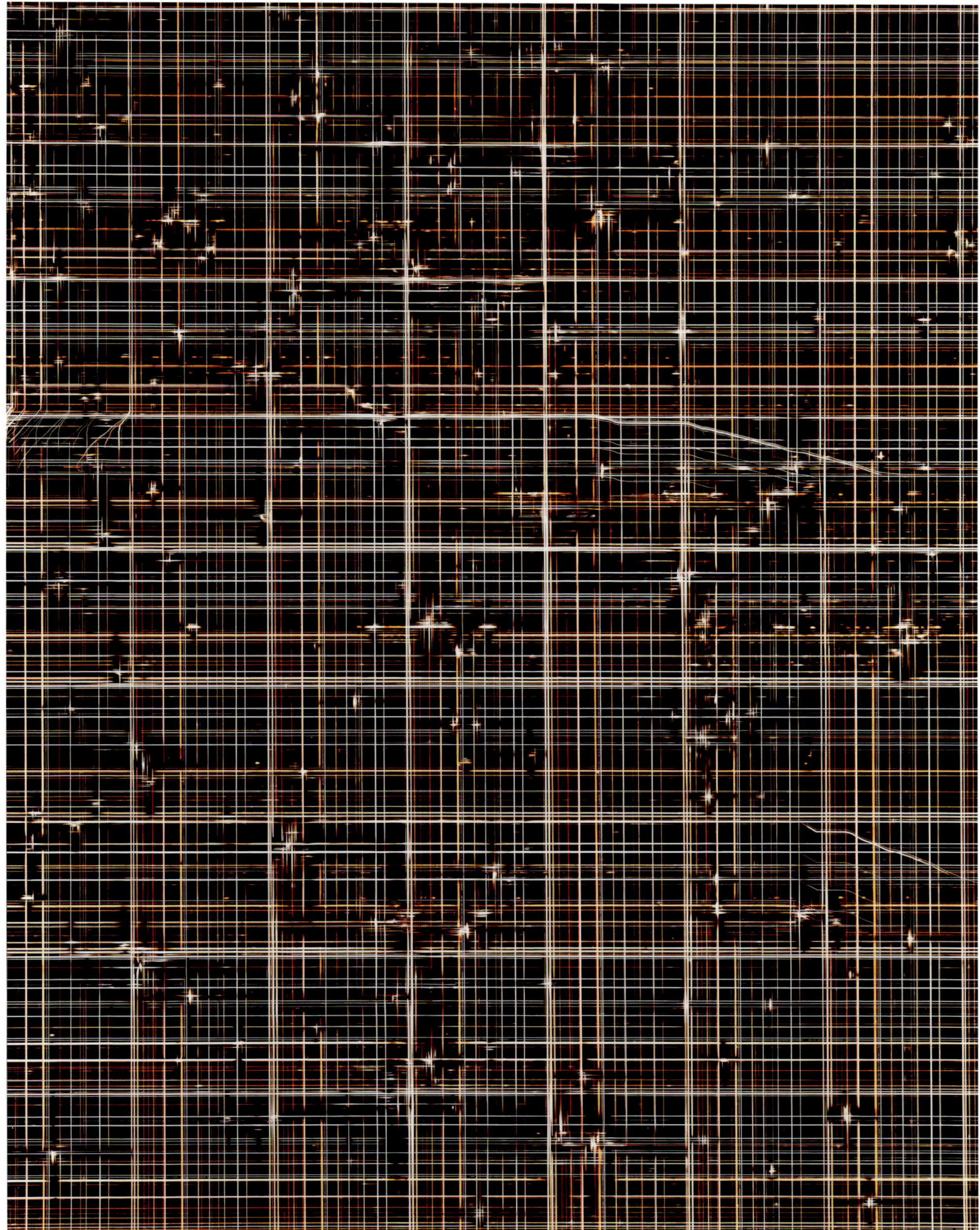

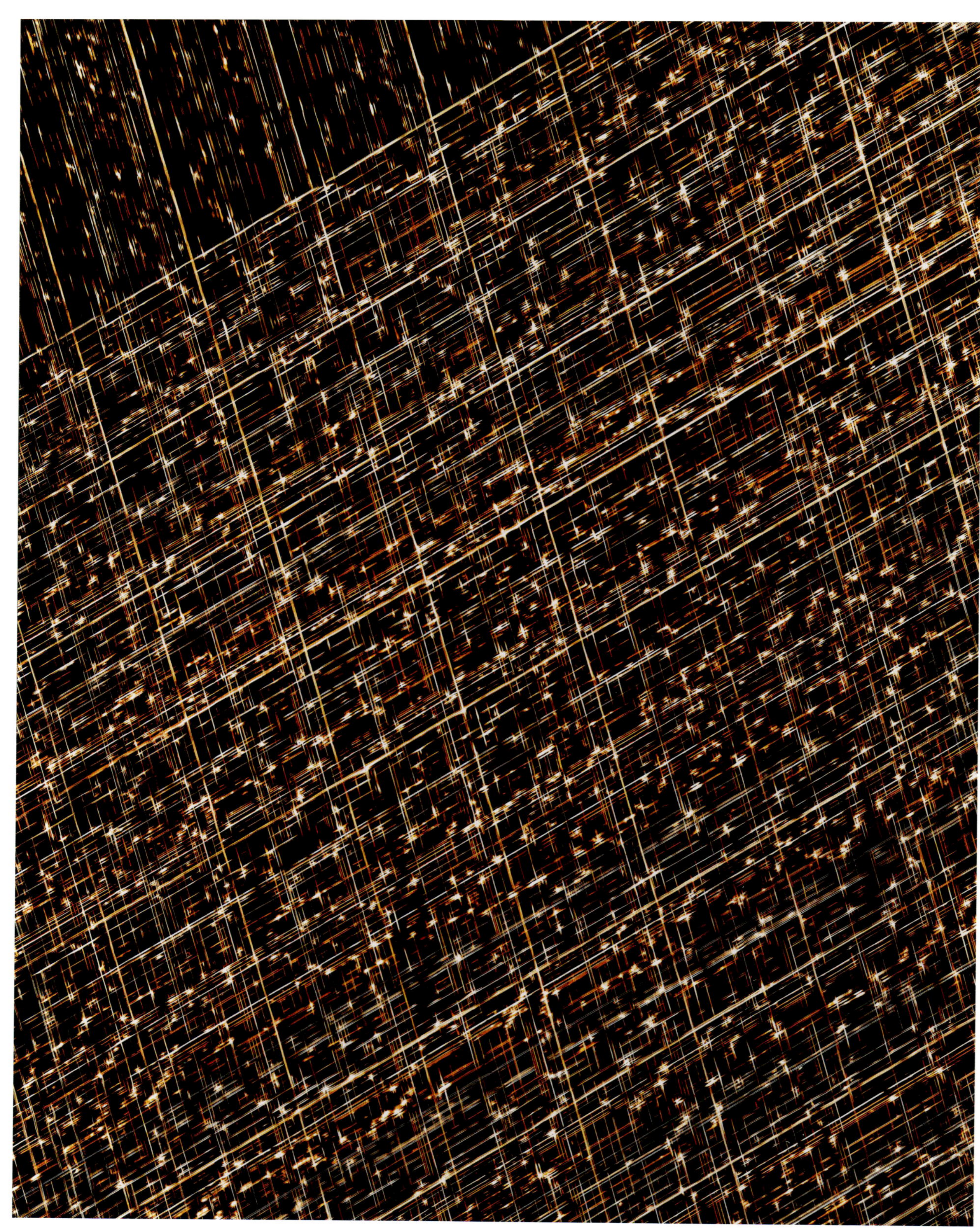

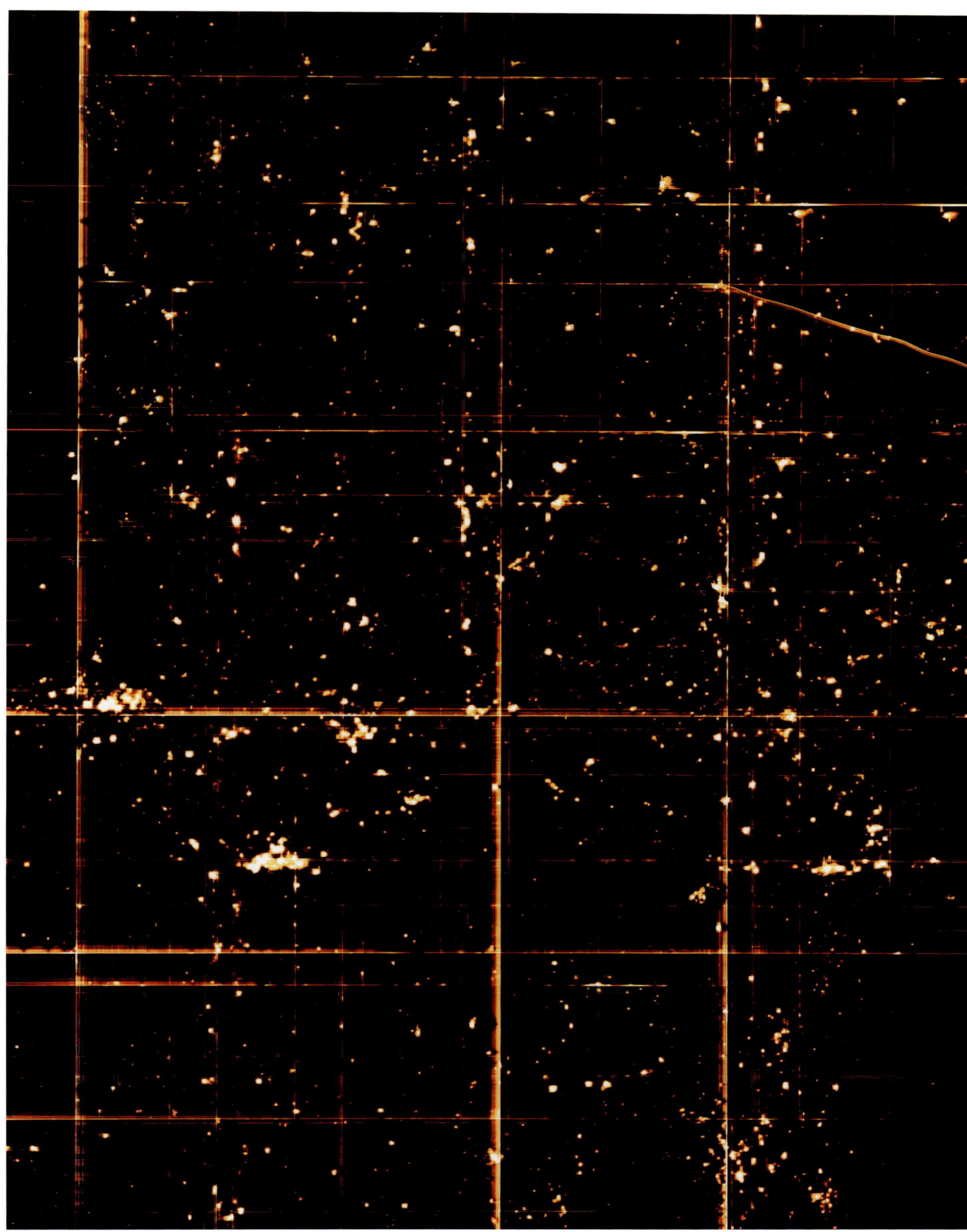

NOTES, QUERIES

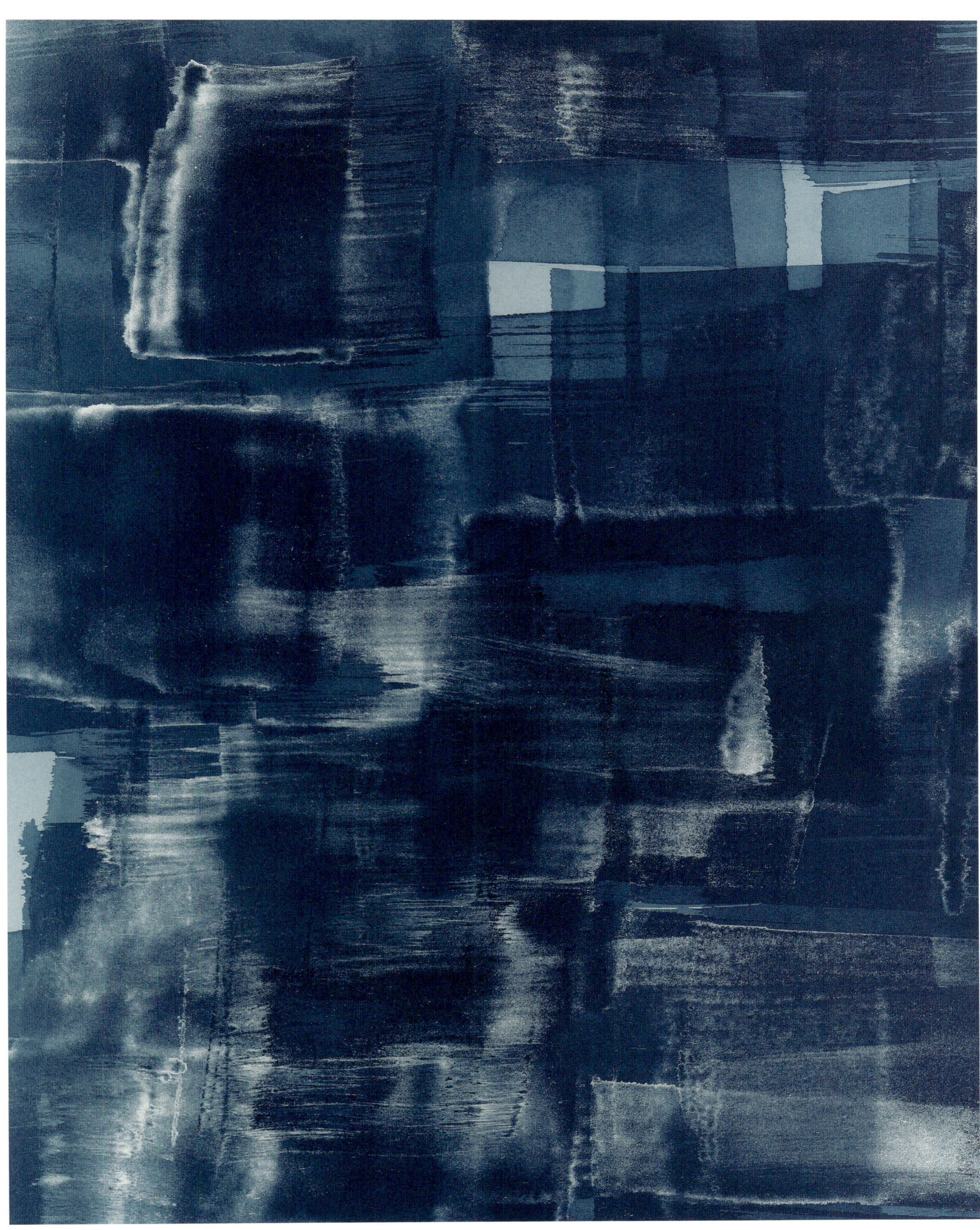

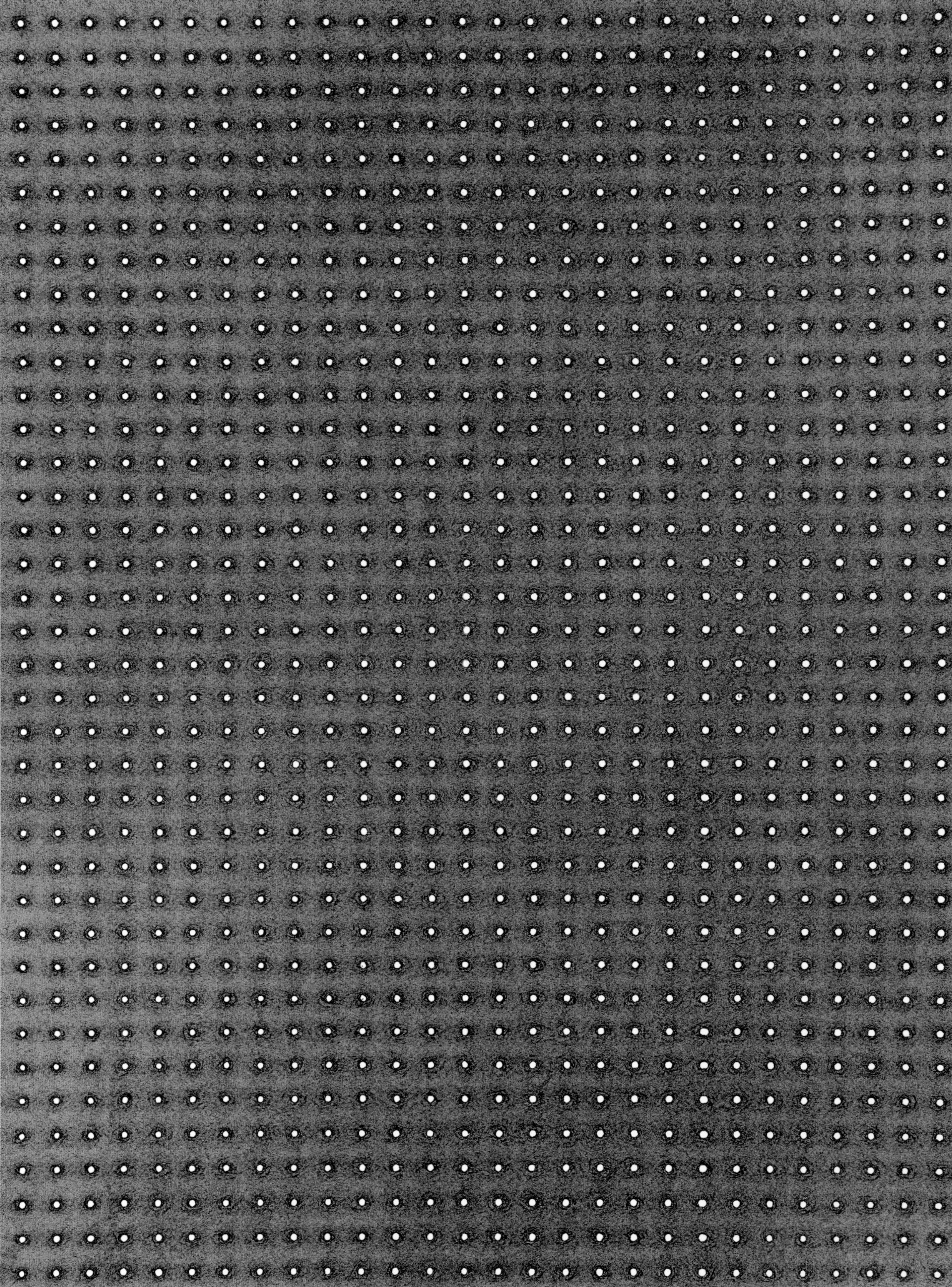

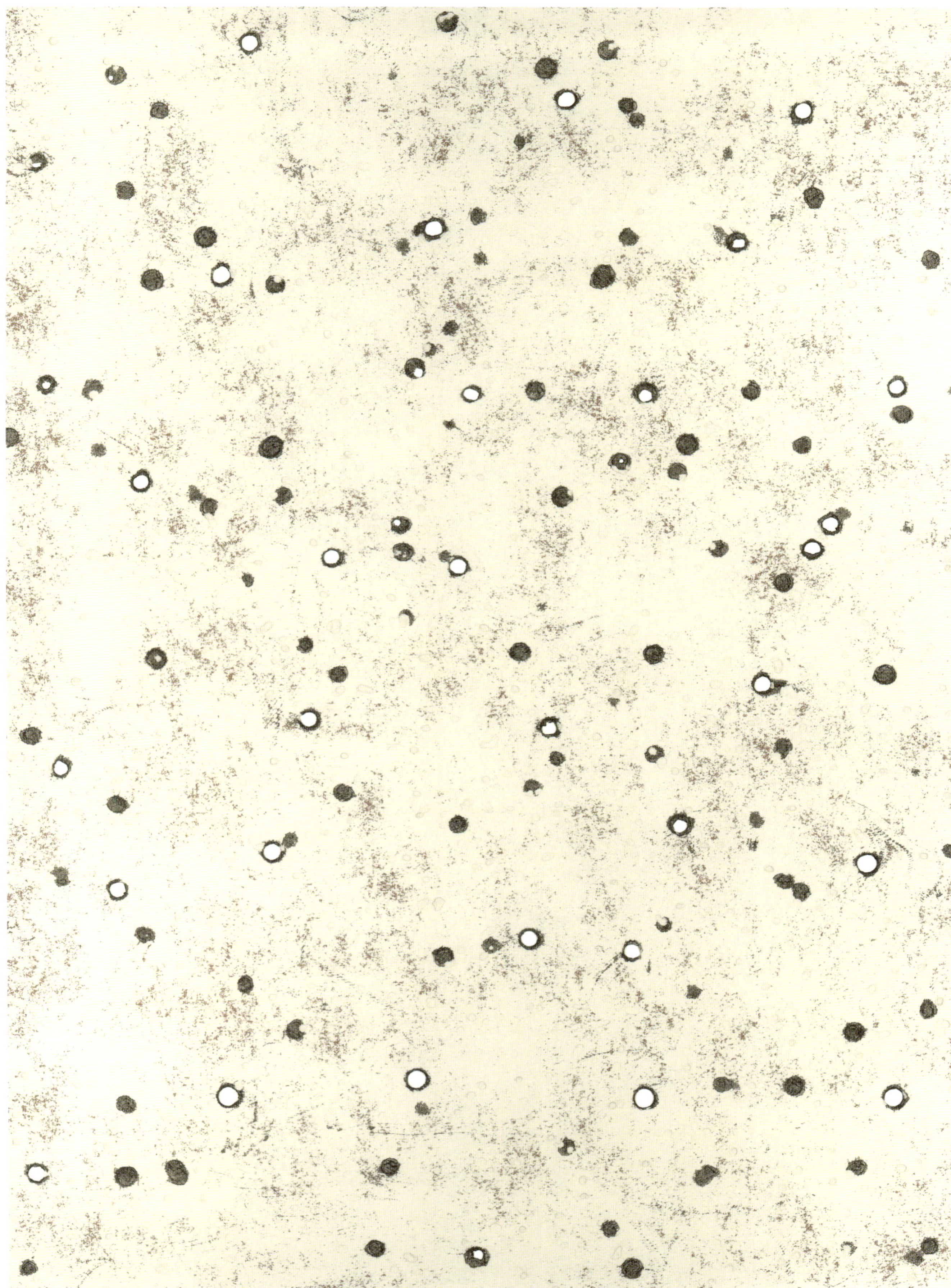

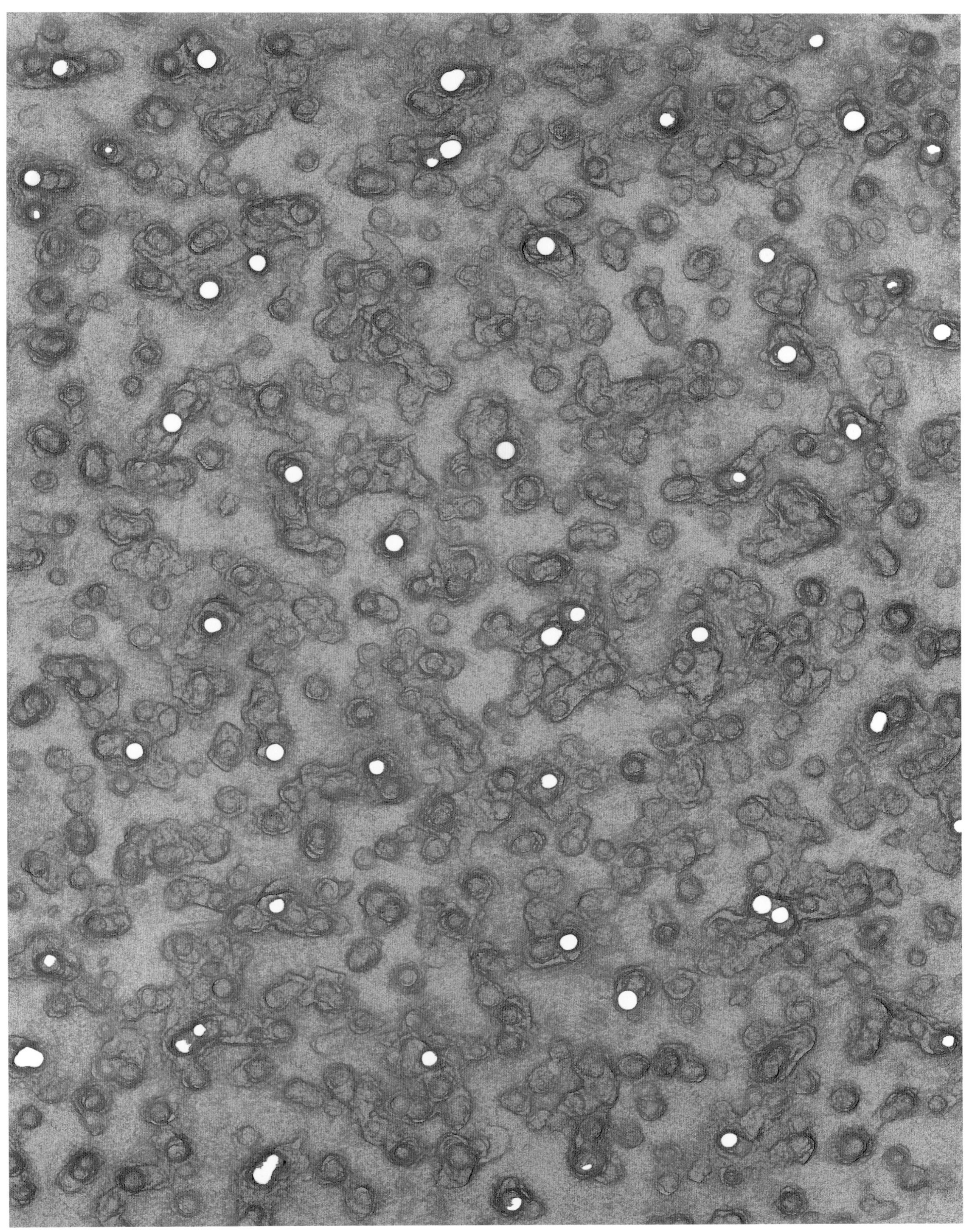

THE MATERIAL IN QUESTION
ESSAY BY MARK ALICE DURANT

IN MID-2006, I VISITED MARCO BREUER at his storefront studio in Hudson, New York. There, photo boxes, wrapped as carefully as birthday presents, are stacked on sawhorse tables that run the length of the open room. Each box houses its own surprise—many contain early versions of works from the series in this book; others reveal experimental imagery gone awry; still others offer astonishment in small packages, humble spectacles of photographic transformation, such as the eclipse-like image created by drilling a small hole through a roll of unexposed 120 mm film. (Fig. a) This image distills the essence of Breuer's approach; while it resembles a nineteenth-century astronomical photograph, its genesis was inspired by the conceptual and performative approaches of a more recent past.

a
Marco Breuer
Hole, 1998
gelatin-silver paper
7 by 5 inches

Breuer showed me dozens of ink drawings he had made during a six-month residency in Japan. The drawings feature a modified version of *suminagashi*, the traditional marbling technique that uses ink floating on the surface of water. As he does with most processes that are new to him, Breuer was pondering a way to bring its play of chance and control into the realm of the photographic. We thumbed through hundreds of snapshots he had hunted and gathered in the flea markets of Kyoto and Tokyo. He is moved by the aura of the ephemeral and the unexpected power of lost images—images that were once gazed upon by familiar eyes, and that now pass through the hands of strangers.

While this monograph focuses primarily on Breuer's cameraless images, his involvement with the photographic medium is as broad as it is deep. His work includes handmade and small-edition books, pinhole imagery, Xerox manipulations, a vast collection of snapshots, and even a handful of camera-generated self-portraits. All of these seemingly disparate activities are part of Breuer's incessant questioning of the essence of photography, how it works and what it means.

During my visit, the walls of Breuer's studio were bare except for a five-foot patch of white cloth, a remnant of the devore process that Breuer learned at a workshop a few years ago. The cloth, made of cotton thread wrapped around a nylon core, had been stamped using the bottom of a beer bottle covered with a kind of paste. When treated with heat, the paste eats away the cotton, leaving a translucent nylon mark. Prompted by a large industrial fan blowing at one end of the studio, the material undulated in the thick summer air. As it fluttered, imperfect circles of light danced and merged on the white wall, like furtive eyes peering from beneath a veil.

Across the room, a small reproduction from an old medical journal sits atop the wainscoting by Breuer's primary worktable. The diagram demonstrates how to dress a head wound: it shows a bandage

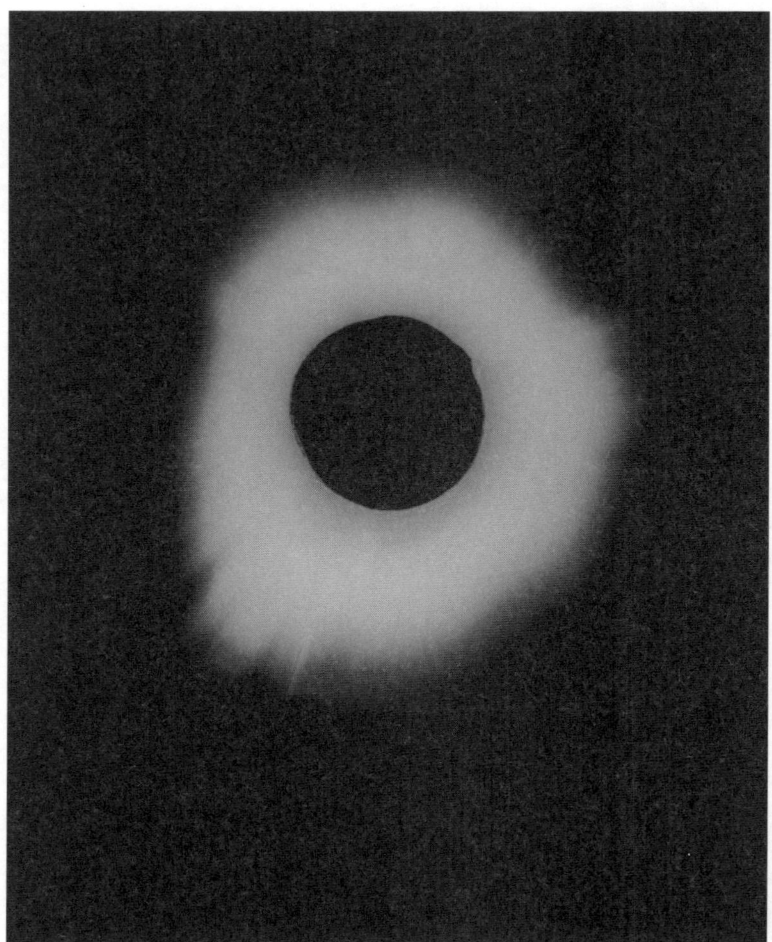

vertically wrapped around a human head as if treating a toothache in the old-fashioned way; the gauze then twists horizontally around the back and front of the head, covering the eyes of the patient.

The world is full of snapshots representing a vast archive of untold things, suggesting innumerable histories whispering on the edge of modern culture. For Breuer, collecting vernacular photographs is an epic curatorial obsession that grants him another way to meditate on the nature of photography. He is attracted to their "objectness"; the more an image has been fingered, creased, smudged, or generally mishandled, the more it draws him. This human patina reinforces Breuer's notion that a photograph continues to be a recording device long after the image leaves the darkroom. Lacking narrative context, the found photograph is loosened from its emotional anchor, and floats like a cheap apparition, familiar yet elusive. When Breuer is not in his studio inventing a language of cameraless photography, he is poking around secondhand stores in search of the jettisoned intimacies of displaced family albums. He "takes" pictures, stalking this quotidian imagery like a street photographer armed with a Leica, on the hunt for the photographable. His extensive pan-cultural collection is organized by sometimes descriptive and sometimes esoteric categories. There is the "Shadow of the Photographer" category, "Man and Beast," "Guys and Guns," "Disembodied Arms Holding Babies," "Plus Fish," and the "Geography of Nowhere" category. He has a large selection of "Cut" images, those emphatically violated frames from which someone or something has been excised for reasons of love or hate. (Fig. b)

In 1985, at the age of nineteen, Breuer moved to Berlin to study at Lette-Verein, a two-year technical photography program. While the noisy and contentious zeitgeist of neo-Expressionism and postmodernism rumbled all around him, Breuer quietly and rigorously studied large-format photography with its emphasis on the "zone system," densitometry, and studio lighting. While this route to photography was rapidly becoming rarefied, if not downright anachronistic, it did give Breuer a deep understanding of materials and processes; the fundamental relationships among light, optics, chemistry, and the sensitivities of emulsions—a body of knowledge that continues to serve him well. After Berlin, he moved to Darmstadt, a former center of the Jugendstil movement, to continue his schooling at the *Fachhochschule*. Although still technically based, his studies broadened to include printmaking, film, and classes in contemporary art and criticism. With a group of fellow art students, Breuer lived and worked in an abandoned doll factory outside of Mannheim. Parties and collaborations ensued—it is hard not to imagine the legions of images and assemblages, like a Hans Bellmer orgy, coming out of that scene.

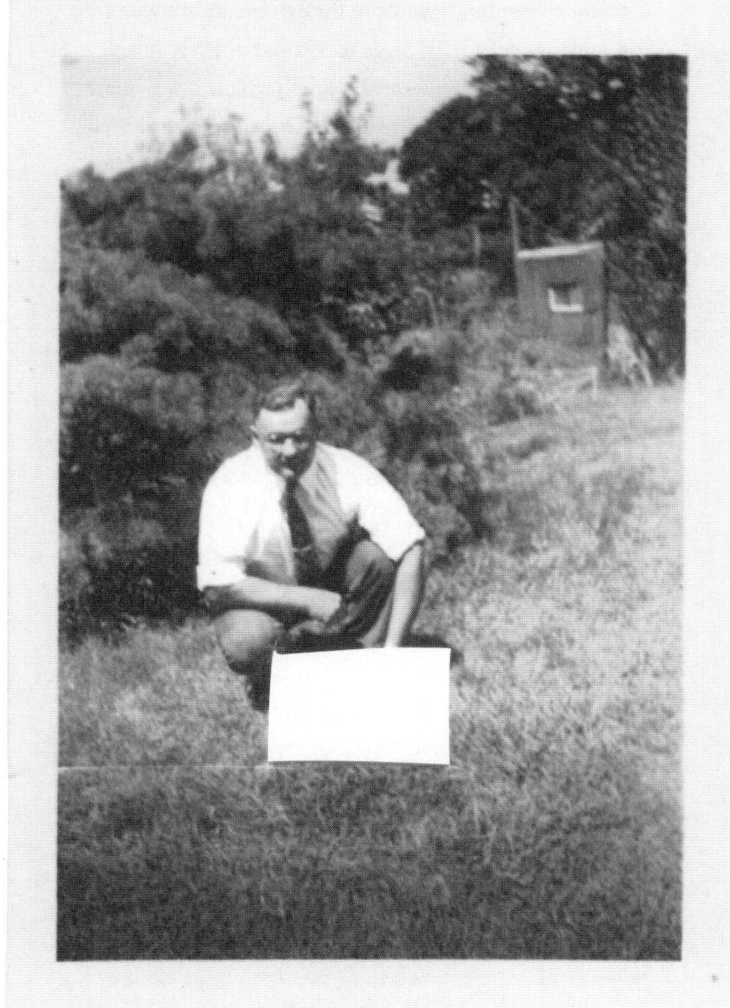

b
found amateur photograph
gelatin-silver paper, cut
3½ by 2½ inches
(collection of Marco Breuer)

After two years in Darmstadt, Breuer traveled to New York City in 1990. It was a fortuitous and revelatory trip, both personally and professionally. While there, he met his future wife Mina Takahashi, and attended papermaking, printmaking, and bookbinding workshops at Dieu Donné Papermill, the Lower East Side Printshop, and the Center for Book Arts; and he discovered the print study room at the Museum of Modern Art. Over the following two years he went back and forth between Germany and the United States, until finally moving permanently to New York in 1993.

Breuer found that Germany and New York presented two distinct modes of working; it was in a sense the difference between the *guild* and the *workshop*. In Germany, whether learning letterpress or silkscreen, one had to apprentice to a master—literally sweeping the floors before being allowed into the inner sanctum. In New York, on the other hand, one could attend weekend workshops to study just about anything. Furthermore, in Germany Breuer was feeling a certain aesthetic claustrophobia in reaction to the growing dominance of the photographers of the Düsseldorf Academy. Spawned by the teachings of Bernd and Hilla Becher, a new generation of German photographers—among them Thomas Ruff, Andreas Gursky, and Thomas Struth—had begun to be the near-exclusive representatives of German photographic practice. And theirs was a style to which Breuer's modest, economical, and more personal works were almost diametrically opposed.

Toward the time of his final project for his Darmstadt degree, Breuer moved to an unheated warehouse in a small border town in the newly opened East Germany. He brought along cameras and photography supplies, and for one hundred days he lived as much as possible outside the daily flux of movies, newspapers, radio, friends, and social life. It was a bohemian paradox: stepping into the remnants of a totalitarian past in order to find freedom. Wanting to dig around in the gray areas of his education, to claim some space in a medium full of rules and strict traditions, Breuer attempted to unravel the tight rigor of his photographic training. It was a lonely and transformative experience, a kind of cultural decompression. As the days passed and winter approached, his rigid striations of working, eating, and sleeping ran together; it became difficult to distinguish "living" time from work time; feeding, cooking, walking were all absorbed into the process of making art. He used household appliances to interfere with the traditional photographic steps of exposure and development. While stoking the wood-burning stove, for example, it occurred to him to subject photographic paper to the glowing embers. He printed multiple self-portraits from a Polaroid negative left for weeks in a holding bath, tracing a kind of material and personal deterioration. Replacing a conventional negative with the badly reproduced instructions for how to use rubber gloves, he slid the scratchy plastic into the enlarger to make a print. He bit down on photo paper and then developed the ghostly dental impressions. He made stereographs that mimicked the way his neighbor's chickens might see the world. And like a modern-day August Sander, he photographed the elderly East German citizens that passed by his temporary studio each day. In the end, a repertoire of procedures had been established, many counterintuitive to photographic tradition, yet photography remained at the heart of these aesthetic wanderings. He assembled a wooden suitcase to house the accumulations of his experiments, an inventory contained in numerous boxes, books, and assorted ephemera distilling his solitary investigations of that hundred days. He carried this Duchampian luggage—evidence of his chrysalis metamorphosis—with him when he moved to New York. That suitcase and its contents,

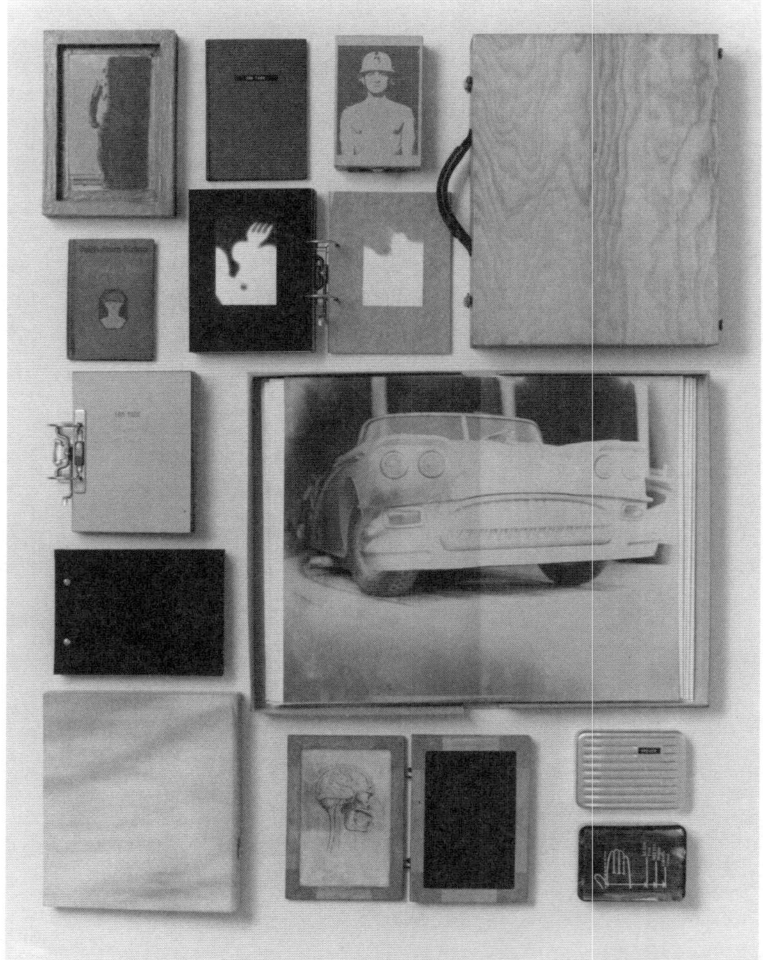

c
Marco Breuer
100 Tage, 1992
mixed media

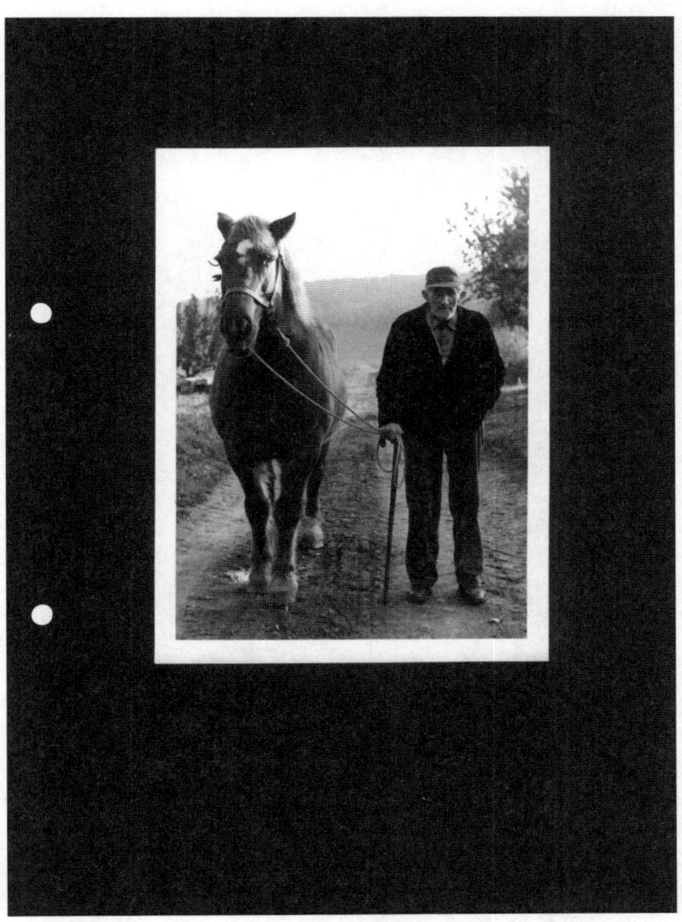

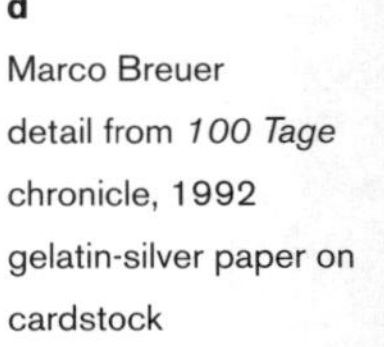

d
Marco Breuer
detail from *100 Tage*
chronicle, 1992
gelatin-silver paper on cardstock
9½ by 7 inches (DIN A5)

now titled *100 Tage* (100 Days), was displayed in his first significant exhibition in New York, *Photography in an Extended Field*, curated by Bill Arning at White Columns the following year. (Figs. c and d)

Like an experimental musician who idolizes Mozart, Breuer is more fiercely attached to photographic history than are many "traditional" photographers. To list the processes and materials in Breuer's work is to take a nonchronological tour through photography's history of material change: from the deep royal blues of cyanotypes and finicky gum bichromate prints of the nineteenth century to the tonal richness of the black-and-white and industrial sheen of machine-processed color papers of the twentieth. Before 1888, when George Eastman proclaimed with his Kodak Brownie camera: "You push the button and we'll do the rest," photography was an unwieldy and time-consuming process. Mid-nineteenth-century photographers were involved in the ongoing invention of the medium; they had to be chemists as well as experts in optics. The sensitivities of emulsions and the quality of lenses, for example, were not yet controlled and regulated by companies such as Kodak, Agfa, and Leica that would come to monopolize twentieth-century photographic tools and materials. But whatever material or technique he is employing, Breuer does not accept the default settings, formats, and recommended procedures of manufactured photographic products.

In an era in which the standard art photograph is a 30-by-40-inch color digital image mounted behind Plexiglas and produced in a limited edition, Breuer's images are remarkable for their modesty of scale and true one-of-a-kind-ness. He has stated: "I like to be in there, physically involved with the image." In that sense, Breuer's sketches have much in common with the characteristics of drawing; the immediacy of the mark and the interaction between the artist's body and surface. For Breuer, working with a negative is working with an old idea, an image from the past; he is concerned not with how photography captures the world but with the unexplored possibilities that lie hidden in the very materiality of photography. Ignited fuses, heat guns, palm sanders, burning swaths of cotton, and X-acto blades are essential tools in Breuer's arsenal. As opposed to analog and digital images, which upon close inspection reveal clumps of granular silver nitrate or jagged pixilations, every mark and trace in Breuer's work holds up under scrutiny. The images in this volume are not distanced representations of an act, but a direct result of the act itself. He interrogates the photographic surface, forcing it to reveal its secrets, and the emulsion reacts as if startled, irritated, perhaps even titillated—as if no one has ever asked these questions before.

This volume, *Early Recordings*, chronicles a wide-ranging selection of Breuer's photo-works from 1996 to 2005. The collection's somewhat ironic title suggests an archaic form of record keeping—wax cylinders featuring scratchy distant voices, or some Rosetta Stone–like artifact that requires deciphering. With all that spitting, biting, burning, and scratching there is a feel of the primitive or primordial in Breuer's processes and procedures. Yet with the complex grids, the improvisatory notations, and visual palimpsests, a conceptual language can be discerned beneath the scarifications and gesticulations. He plays photography like a John Cage piano. For Breuer, the temporality of photography is not limited to the shutter's

e
Marco Breuer
Study for *Untitled (Artificial Light)*, 2000
16 mm, b/w, silent

fraction-of-a-second exposure. He is interested in stretching the sense of time that can exist in its recording life; it might take minutes, hours, days to "complete" an image. It is as if he traveled back to the early nineteenth century armed with an understanding of Conceptual art and a belief in the possibilities of chance operations, in order to reinvent photography, or at least offer another path that is not slave to the camera and its presumed optical certainties.

A handful of Breuer's hybrid photograms opens this book, and acts as a portal into his world of photographic phenomena. Despite the technique's apparent irreducibility, Breuer has found ways to re-imagine the basic language of the photogram, even reviving the obscure subcategory "luminogram"—an image made with light only. Some are "stealth photograms," that is, when hair, spit, bread, clear tape, or an air-conditioning filter were fitted in the enlarger where a negative is normally placed; with these, the resulting image shifts the scale of the host object and yet retains the one-to-one object-image relationship. Other photograms are self-referential, documenting the act of their own making: *E/Z (Light)* is an image/record of a light bulb being quickly switched on and off as it sat upon photographic paper. Revisiting a method from his *100 Tage* project, in *Untitled (Coals)* the photo paper is subjected to the red glow of coals, mapping the topography of the burning charcoal. *Untitled (Alc./99%)* reveals a sensuous time-exposure catalyzed by pouring rubbing alcohol and setting it aflame, the burning and evaporating liquid coaxes seemingly impossible colors and tonalities from the black-and-white emulsion.

The works that comprise the sections Pan and Tilt, Time Being, and Complications (Problem I–IV) represent Breuer's shift in 2002 from black and white to chromogenic paper (the standard photo paper for most contemporary color photographs). In a kind of reverse frottage he limits his actions to sanding and scratching, abrading the surface to get to the layers of color below. On occasion he loops this subtractive process by making contact prints from previous images and in the back and forth of sanding/contacting, reveals unusual hues and subtle transformations in focus and sharpness. The idea of the seemingly precise vertical and horizontal lines found in Pan and

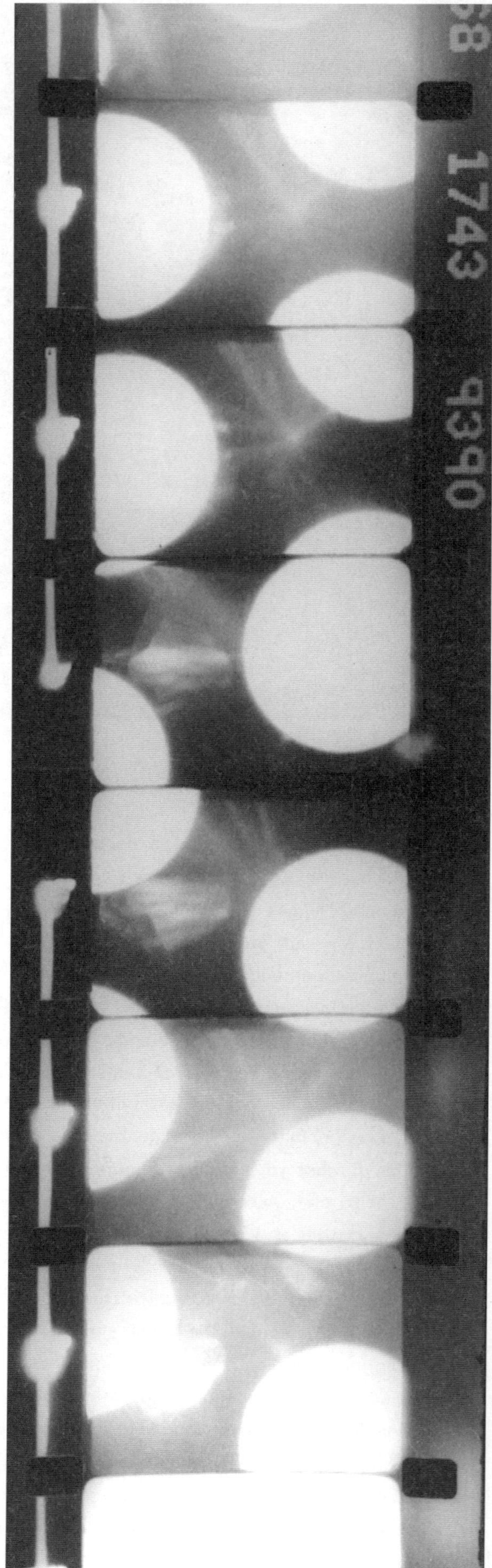

Tilt was stimulated by his experiments with 16 mm movie film and the inevitable scratches the film gathers when it repeatedly passes through a projector. (Fig. e) Starting with an exposed and processed sheet of paper, the ruler-guided blade effaces the mute black surface, accessing yellow and red dyes and the white tooth of the paper base. When encountering small bumps from the dust and particles beneath the paper, the precision of the scratched line is interrupted, creating multiple visual events that appear like terrestrial explosions viewed from orbit or double-shadowed mountains illuminated by dueling suns. The effect is stunning: our eyes travel along lines of latitude, longitude, and altitude, suggesting the running blur of a movie when it slides out of the projector's gate, or perhaps time-lapse images of the movement of Saturn's rings. The perceptual leap—from the scored surface of photographic emulsion to the dramatic spectacles the images suggest—is a testament to the paradox of gesture and effect in Breuer's works. He demonstrates that a simple material and procedural act can yield extraordinarily complex metaphorical results.

For the series Notes, Queries, exhibited at Von Lintel Gallery in 2005–6, Breuer set out to reverse the subtractive process of the Pan and Tilt series and work with an additive color process. Looking back to when photography was still in its protean infancy, Breuer embraced nineteenth-century techniques of cyanotype and gum bichromate, both of which require hand-application of the emulsion onto absorbent paper. The astronomer John Herschel invented the cyanotype process with its celestial blues in 1842. In Breuer's approach, the emulsion is applied in patches or in drips but always in a manner that presents the variable hues of the process not as vehicle to an image but as image itself. Paradoxically at times the density of the layering process prevents exposure, negating the cyanotype's light sensitivity. In the case of the gum bichromate prints, multiple layers of the gum arabic imbued with watercolor pigment and a sensitizer are necessary to attain color density. After exposure to ultraviolet light, the gum prints are developed and left to dry. The prints are then physically reworked and again coated with emulsion. This process of layering and sanding is repeated over several days as the images continue to record the dance between nurturance and violation, presence and negation. These patterns of stained and scarred surfaces, suggesting landscapes that have experienced both organic and manufactured phenomena, hint at ideas of absorption and resistance of a different order. Breuer does not mystify his process or his materials; he is quite clear about their manufacture. He does not mythologize himself or his work: in conversation he never veers far from the material in question and refuses to romanticize his imagery. Nevertheless, while he works within the narrow parameters of each individual material, revealing the hidden layers of blindness and sensitivity of his recording devices, these works in particular betray the artist's sensitivity to the tortured and wounded terrestrial skins of our own era of incessant violence.

The photograph is both the vehicle and the site of a fairly complex series of optical/chemical processes that remain outside the frame. There is a putative "transparency" to the medium: photographs hide themselves in order to reveal the world. In Breuer's imagery, the physical manifestation of the photograph as we have come to expect it—that is, the unencumbered window to the concrete world of things—does not exist. There is not even the dirty window of veiling, masking, and toning effects that so many artist/photographers employ in order to create a patina for their images. The industrial shellac that is a photograph's emulsion is the location of and complicit witness to the acts Breuer performs upon them. Without relying on decorative or distorting painterly or sculptural effects, Breuer's gesticulations mark a surface that asks for no marks; they are records of private performances, and as such they are evidence not of the world as seen through the lens, but of the artist's direct interaction with the photographic material. All marks, however humble or tentative, are exclamatory. A trace, by contrast, may be involuntary, as a fleeting shadow upon a wall suggests a temporary presence.

Photography attempts to foil impermanence; this is why photography has been called "the art of fixing a shadow" (an expression coined by William Henry Fox Talbot), and seems forever weighted by melancholy. As Roland Barthes has suggested, the basic gesture of photography is *to point*, but it is always pointing to something in the past. "That was there" is a sentiment underlying almost all photographs. In radical opposition to this tradition, Breuer's images are not haunted; indeed, they are bracingly free of longing. There is no intermediary device to distance image and event. These are not images that a camera can make. They do not indulge in nostalgia; there are no vague, diaphanous, fuzzy-edged, vignette'ed evocations of memory, the past, or ghostliness. Nor does Breuer rely on emptied-out appropriations. He has no faith in inflated narratives or visual non sequiturs. He has no parasitic relation to content; these are not concerned, outraged, or cynical documents of the human condition. They are free of explicit sociopolitical agenda, free of lenses and shadows, free of mirrors and windows, free of an immodesty of scale; they are free of the whole tired argument about the burden of representation.

Breuer's work is fundamentally different in his insistence that photography need not be ruled by the tyranny of the camera, and as he learns each new approach and process he somehow finds a way for it to be folded back into the realm of photographic phenomena in his attempt to rediscover for himself the history and material essence of the medium. As Geoffrey Batchen has explored in his varied histories of photography, the invention of photography in the late 1830s (popularly attributed to the Frenchman Louis Daguerre, with a secondary nod to the Englishman Talbot) was preceded by rampant experimentation with light-sensitive emulsions throughout the seventeenth and eighteenth centuries. Breuer makes no claims to originality, stating: "Art history is too obsessed with invention. I don't claim to invent anything because there is a good chance it has been done in the 1960s, or the '20s, or the 1830s"; still, his work hints at paths not taken in photography's inchoate early development.

Imagine a collaboration between Talbot and artist Sol LeWitt (who himself was influenced by Eadweard Muybridge's nineteenth-century studies in animal locomotion) and what you conjure may look something like the images in this book. One of Breuer's self-portraits in particular suggests this hypothetical collaboration between nineteenth-century photographer/inventor and contemporary Conceptualist. (Fig. f) Breuer appears to be wearing a formal suit while carrying an empty chair upon his back. Although the camera turns toward the artist, the artist turns away from the camera. The figure is reminiscent of one of those intrepid Victorian photographers who mounted their cameras and portable darkrooms upon their backs as they scaled mountains and scrambled through jungles. Without a horizon line to place the figure, it is difficult

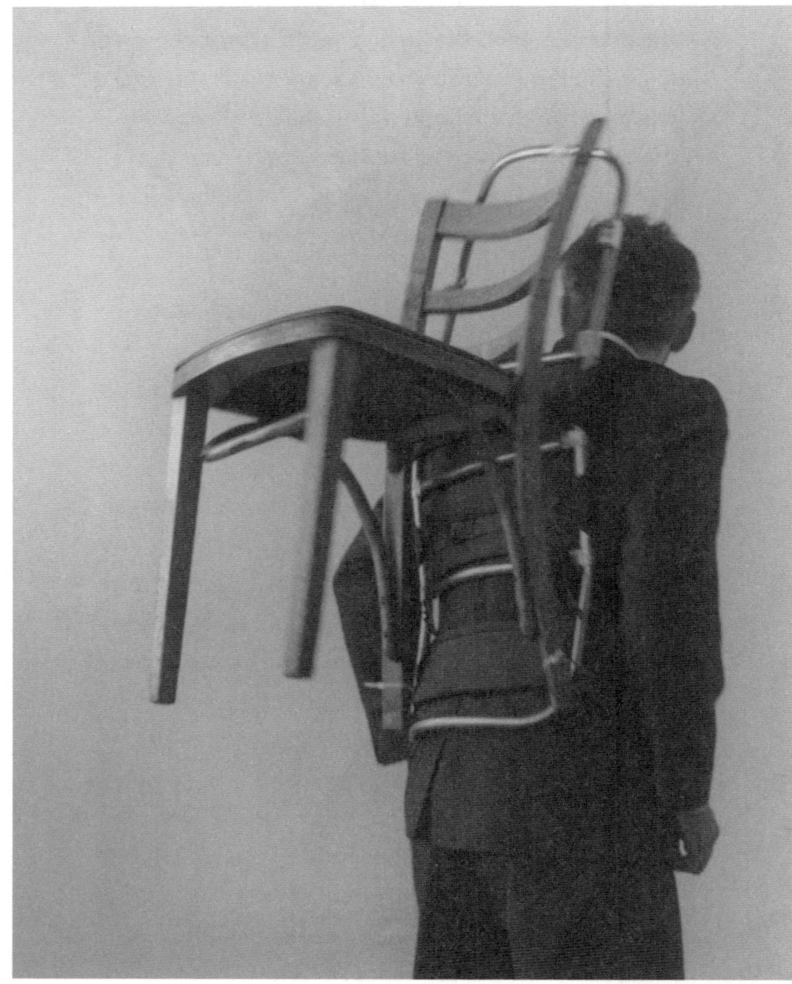

f
Marco Breuer
Untitled (Chair), 1999
from *For Now*
gelatin-silver paper
7 by 5 inches

to tell if he is on a mountaintop or a glacier, if he stands in thick fog or an empty studio. The image is inscrutable: slapstick and elegant, resistant yet resonant. Perhaps Breuer's suitcase from *100 Tage* sits at his feet, waiting to be reopened to reveal long-suppressed secrets from the history of photography. Is he facing forward or backward? Is that empty chair for us?

It is not at all unusual for painters to do performance, for performance artists to make paintings, for sculptors to work with sound, for photographers

to manually or digitally manipulate their images, and at this particular moment in contemporary art it seems that almost *every* artist makes video installations. Artists are at liberty to use whatever medium is appropriate to their ideas, and few would argue to restrict the freedom of that interdisciplinary spirit. Yet by shifting media the artist trades one set of problems for another; often the lateral move to a different medium represents an avoidance or even a retreat from the awkward dance between an artist's intentions and the thorny resistance of materials. Believing that mystery and discovery still play hide-and-seek close to home, Breuer would argue that it is at that very point of resistance that things get interesting. By avoiding the vagaries of mixed media and insisting that the basic materiality of photography be the site of his formal and procedural investigations, Breuer creates work that is maverick in an era of facile interdisciplinarity. The history of photography is inevitably tied to people, places, and things; through his gesticulations and calculations, an accumulation of vital gestures, Breuer surrenders specificities in order to renegotiate the medium's relation to the real. In his hands, corpus photography may be pale, pitted, bitten, scratched, punctured, smoked, and singed, but unlocked by these sometimes brief, sometimes extended moments of action, the surface/image is transformed from a field of scars into a radiant terrain.

MARK ALICE DURANT is a professor in the Department of Visual Arts at the University of Maryland, Baltimore. His writing has appeared in *Art in America*, *Exposure*, and *Afterimage*, among other publications. He has contributed to several monographs, including *Vik Muniz: Seeing Is Believing* and is co-author, most recently, of *Blur of the Otherworldly: Contemporary Art, Technology, and the Paranormal.*

MARCO BREUER was born in Landshut, Germany in 1966. He has exhibited internationally, and his work is in numerous collections, including the Museum of Modern Art, New York; New York Public Library; San Francisco Museum of Modern Art; Museum of Fine Arts, Boston; and Staatsgalerie in Stuttgart, Germany. Breuer is the recipient of many awards and honors, including a Guggenheim fellowship (2006), a Japan-US Friendship Commission/NEA Creative Artists Exchange Fellowship (2005), a Carriage House Residency at the Islip Art Museum (2004), a Peter S. Reed Foundation Grant (2000) and three MacDowell Colony residencies (2000, 2001, 2003). His publication *SMTWTFS* received wide critical acclaim and the *Photo-eye* Award for Best Photography Book of 2002. He is represented by Von Lintel Gallery in New York City. Breuer lives in upstate New York.

Sources

Geoffrey Batchen, *Burning with Desire: The Conception of Photography* (Cambridge, MA: MIT Press, 1999)

Jacqueline Brody, "Marco Breuer, Counting in Circles," *Art on Paper* (September/October 2001)

Catherine de Zegher, ed., *The Stage of Drawing: Gesture and Act* (London, New York: Tate Publishing and the Drawing Center, 2003)

1
Untitled (Bag), 1998
gelatin-silver paper
8 by 6 inches, unique

2
Untitled (Hair), 1996
gelatin-silver paper
8 by 6 inches, unique

3
Untitled (Filter), 1998
gelatin-silver paper
8 by 6 inches, unique

4
Untitled (Up), 1998
gelatin-silver paper, scratched
8 by 6 inches, unique

5
Untitled (Alc./99%), 1999
gelatin-silver paper, burned
8 by 6 inches, unique

6
E/Z (Bites), 1996
gelatin-silver paper, chewed
11 by 8½ inches, unique

7
E/Z (Spit), 1996
gelatin-silver paper
13 by 10 inches, unique

8
E/Z (Toast), 1996
gelatin-silver paper
13 by 10 inches, unique

9
E/Z (Cuts/500), 1996
gelatin-silver paper, cut
19½ by 15⅜ inches, unique

10
E/Z (Cuts/Less), 1996
gelatin-silver paper
19½ by 15⅜ inches, unique

11
Untitled (Light), 1999
gelatin-silver paper
11 by 8½ inches, unique

12
Untitled (Tape), 1998
gelatin-silver paper
11 by 8½ inches, unique

13
Untitled (Brush), 1999
gelatin-silver paper, brushed
11 by 8½ inches, unique

14
Untitled (Fall), 2000
gelatin-silver paper, burned
11 by 8½ inches, unique

15
Untitled (Move), 2001
gelatin-silver paper, burned
11 by 8½ inches, unique

16
Untitled (Heat/Gun), 2000
gelatin-silver paper, burned
11 by 8½ inches, unique

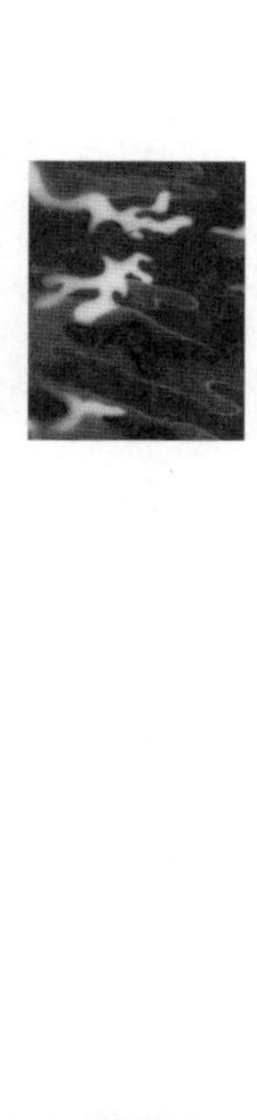
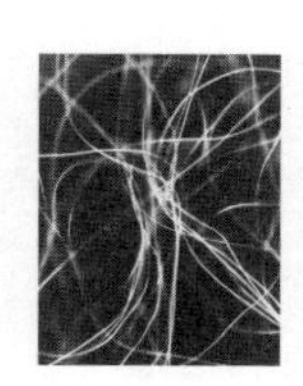
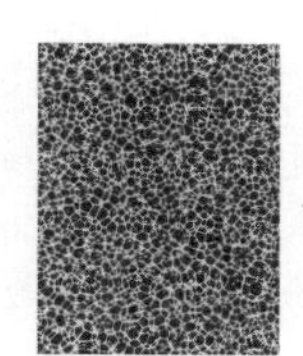
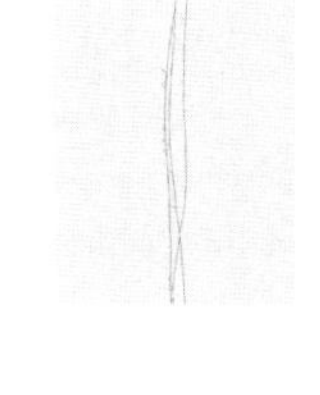
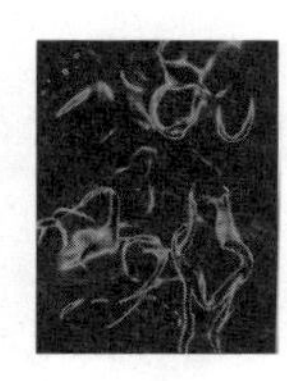
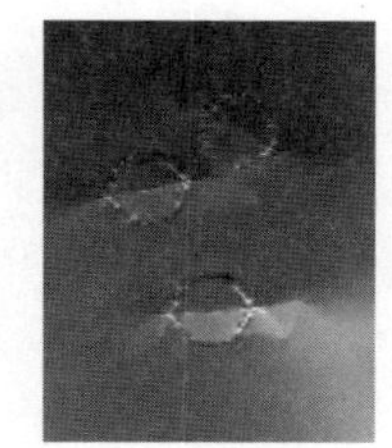
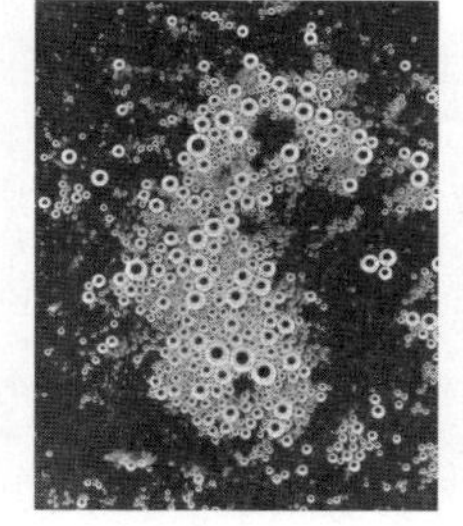
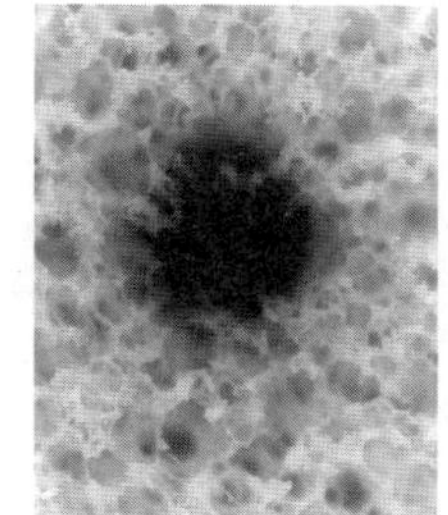
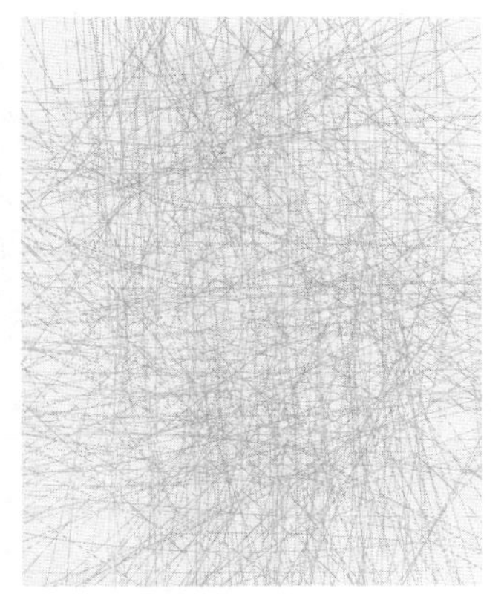
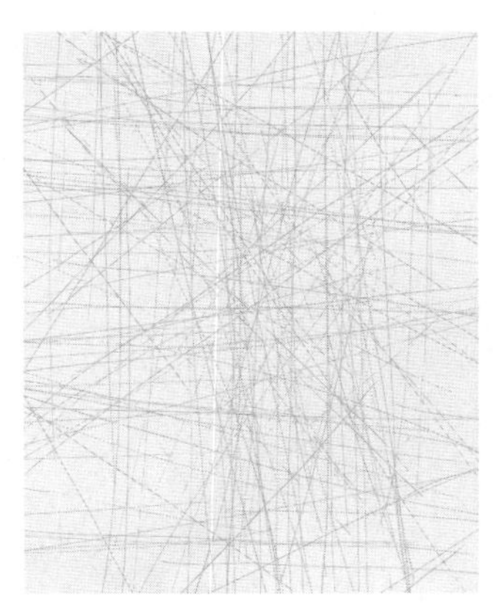
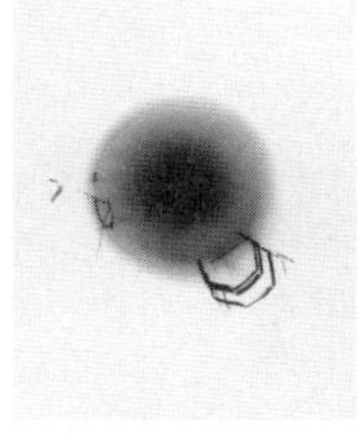
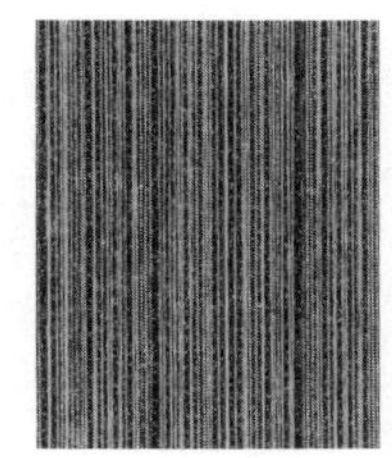
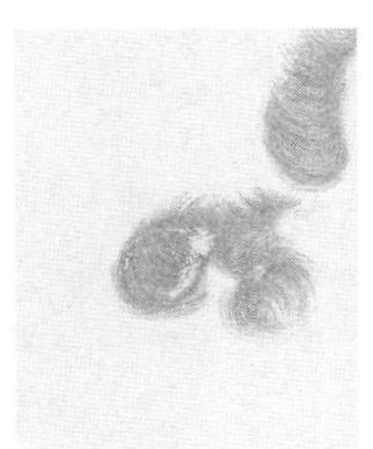
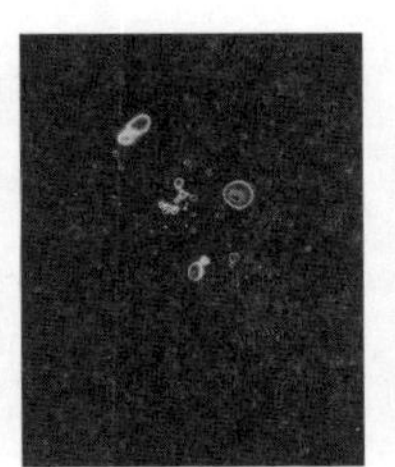
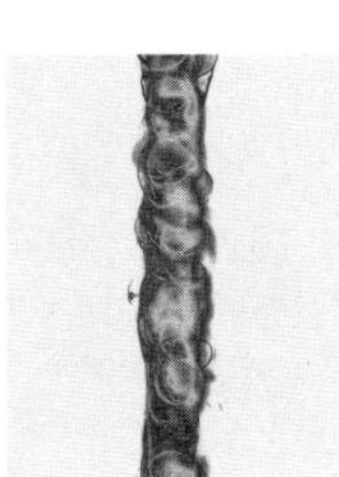
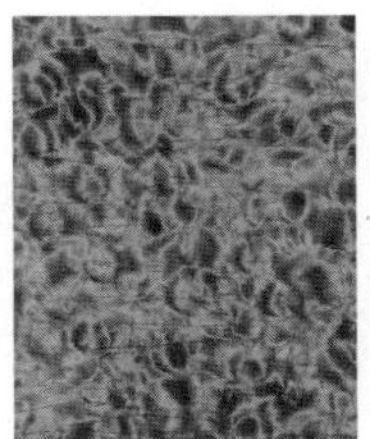

17
Untitled (Fold), 2001
gelatin-silver paper, folded/sanded
11 by 8½ inches, unique

18
Untitled (Abrasive), 1996
gelatin-silver paper, sanded
19½ by 15 11/16 inches, unique

19
Untitled (Coals), 1996
gelatin-silver paper, burned
19½ by 15 11/16 inches, unique

20
Untitled (Coals), 1996
gelatin-silver paper, burned
19½ by 15 11/16 inches, unique

21
Untitled (Coals), 1996
gelatin-silver paper, burned
19½ by 15 11/16 inches, unique

22
Untitled (Fuse), 1996
gelatin-silver paper, burned
18 by 14 inches, unique

23
Untitled (Sparks), 1997
gelatin-silver paper, burned
18 by 14 inches, unique

24
Untitled (100% Cotton), 1999
gelatin-silver paper, burned
18 by 14 inches, unique

25
Untitled (100% Cotton), 1999
gelatin-silver paper, burned
18 by 14 inches, unique

26
Untitled (Palm), 1999
gelatin-silver paper, sanded
18 by 14 inches, unique

27
Untitled (Palm), 1999
gelatin-silver paper, sanded
18 by 14 inches, unique

28
Pan (C-270), 2003
chromogenic paper, scratched
23⅝ by 19⅝ inches, unique

29
Pan (C-362), 2003
chromogenic paper, scratched
23¾ by 19⅝ inches, unique

30
Tilt (C-411), 2004
chromogenic paper, scratched
23 5/16 by 19½ inches, unique

31
Tilt (C-371), 2003
chromogenic paper, scratched
23 1/16 by 19⅛ inches, unique

32
Pan (C-379), 2003
chromogenic paper, scratched
23 11/16 by 19 11/16 inches, unique

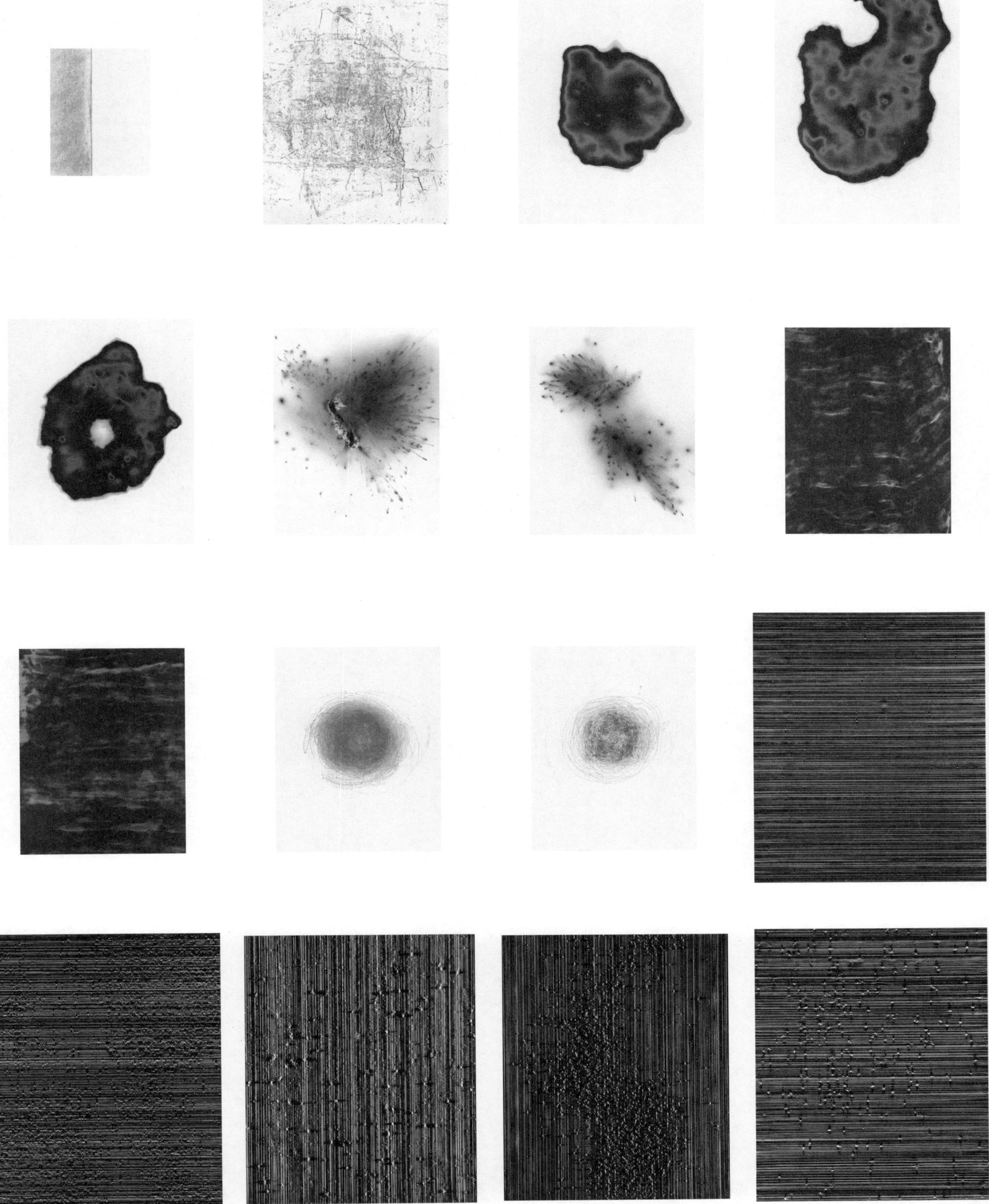

33
Untitled (C-287), 2003
chromogenic paper, scratched
13½ by 10½ inches, unique

34
Untitled (C-281), 2003
chromogenic paper, scratched
13¾ by 10⅝ inches, unique

35
Untitled (C-349), 2003
chromogenic paper, scratched
13 11/16 by 10 11/16 inches, unique

36
Untitled (C-357), 2003
chromogenic paper, scratched
13⅝ by 10¾ inches, unique

37
Untitled (C-498), 2004
chromogenic paper, scratched
13¾ by 10 11/16 inches, unique

38
Untitled (C-295), 2003
chromogenic paper, scratched
13⅞ by 10⅝ inches, unique

39
Untitled (C-314), 2003
chromogenic paper, scratched
13¾ by 10 11/16 inches, unique

40
Untitled (C-367), 2003
chromogenic paper, scratched
13 11/16 by 10 9/16 inches, unique

41
Untitled (E-33), 2005
cyanotype on Fabriano paper
15 11/16 by 12⅜ inches, unique

42
Untitled (E-41), 2005
cyanotype on Fabriano paper, folded
18½ by 14½ inches, unique

43
Untitled (E-100), 2005
gum bichromate on Fabriano paper, folded/abraded
18 15/16 by 14¼ inches, unique

44
Untitled (E-126), 2005
gum bichromate on Fabriano paper, abraded
18 9/16 by 13 5/16 inches, unique

45
Untitled (E-106), 2005
gum bichromate over cyanotype on Fabriano paper, abraded
18 11/16 by 13½ inches, unique

46
Untitled (E-157), 2005
cyanotype on Arches paper
17¼ by 13⅜ inches, unique

47
Untitled (E-117), 2005
gum bichromate on Fabriano paper, abraded
18⅜ by 14 inches, unique

48
Untitled (E-97), 2005
gum bichromate on Fabriano paper, abraded
18 3/16 by 14 inches, unique

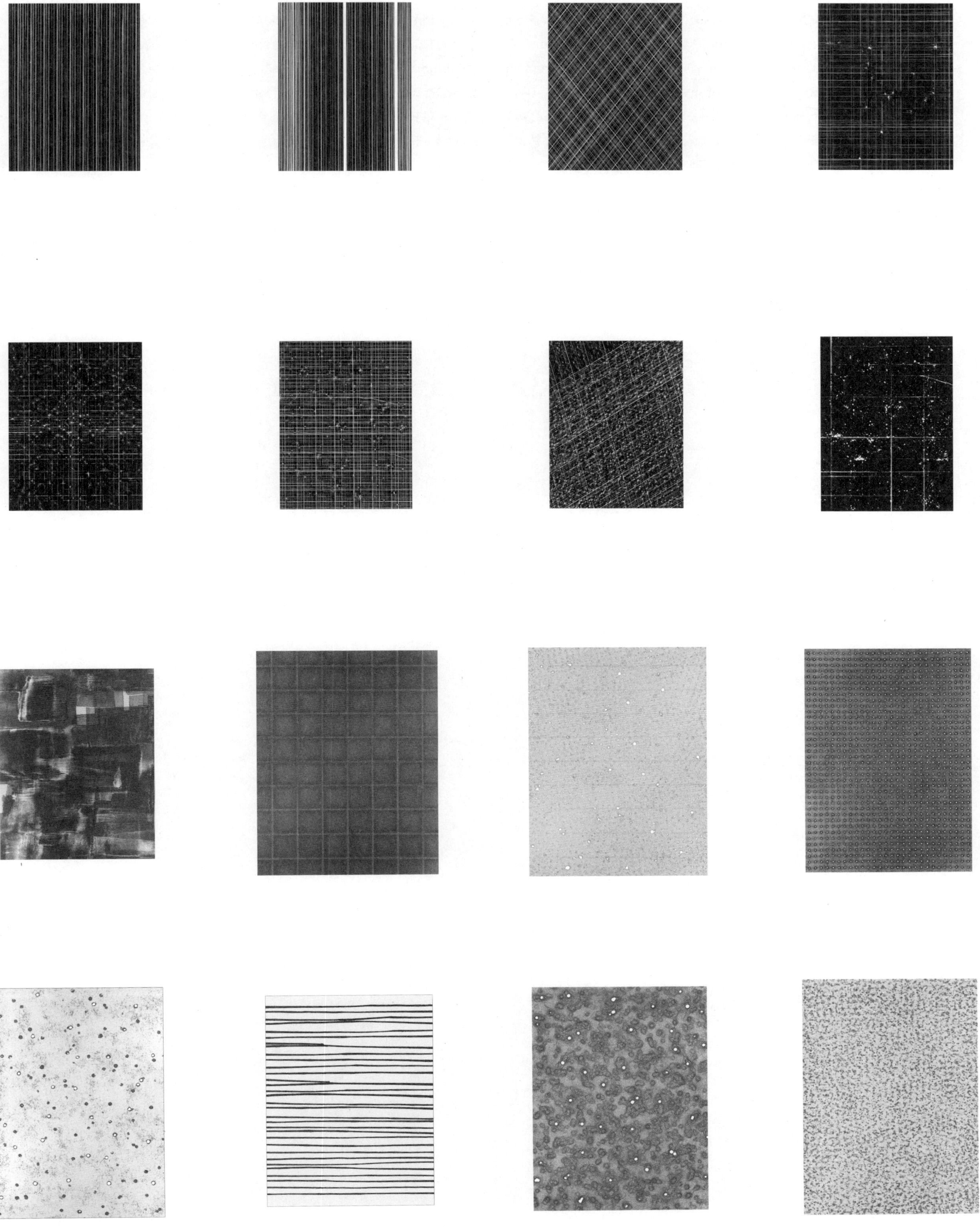

MARCO BREUER THANKS Lesley Martin, Andrew Sloat, Matthew Pimm, Martin Senn, Mark Alice Durant, Isabella Breuer, Denise Breuer, Mina Takahashi, Ami Takahashi, Thomas Von Lintel, Collette Blanchard, Natasha Ogilvie, Nick Lamia, John Tevis, Arnold Helbling, Oona Stern, James Carl, James Hegge, Stephen Frailey, Tim Davis, Mitch Epstein, Lynne Tillman, Jeffrey DeShell, Peter Cameron, Piper Shepard, E.E. Smith, Steven Brower, Tilman Reichert, Jens Ziehe, Uli Bohnen, Hans Hansen, Chuck Mobley, Susan Kismaric, Peter Galassi, Vince Aletti, Bill Arning, Martha Buskirk, Virginia Heckert, Mark Sloan, Brett Littman, Jacqueline Brody, Bobby Rainwater, Gisela Floto, Celina Lunsford, John Simon Guggenheim Memorial Foundation, MacDowell Colony.

Endpaper: *Pan (C-270), 2003*

Editor: Lesley A. Martin
Designer: Andrew Sloat
Production: Matthew Pimm

The staff for this book at Aperture Foundation includes:
Ellen S. Harris, *Executive Director*; Michael Culoso, *Director of Finance and Administration*; Nancy Grubb, *Executive Managing Editor, Books*; Susan Ciccotti, *Production Editor*; Andrea Smith, *Director of Communications*; Kristian Orozco, *Director of Sales and Foreign Rights*; Diana Edkins, *Director of Exhibitions and Limited-Edition Photographs*; Elliot Black and Daoud Tyler-Ameen, *Work Scholars*

First edition
Printed and bound in Italy
10 9 8 7 6 5 4 3 2 1

Library of Congress Control Number: 2006934555
ISBN 978-1-59711-033-4

Aperture Foundation books are available in North America through:
D.A.P./Distributed Art Publishers
155 Sixth Avenue, 2nd Floor
New York, N.Y. 10013
Phone: (212) 627-1999
Fax: (212) 627-9484

Aperture Foundation books are distributed outside North America by:
Thames & Hudson
181A High Holborn
London WC1V 7QX
United Kingdom
Phone: + 44 20 7845 5000
Fax: + 44 20 7845 5055
Email: sales@thameshudson.co.uk

aperturefoundation
547 West 27th Street
New York, N.Y. 10001
www.aperture.org

The purpose of Aperture Foundation, a non-profit organization, is to advance photography in all its forms and to foster the exchange of ideas among audiences worldwide.